S0-BDA-086

best sex writing
2005

best sex writing 2005

Edited by Violet Blue

CLEIS
PRESS

Copyright © 2005 by Violet Blue.

All rights reserved. Except for brief passages quoted in newspaper, magazine, radio, or television reviews, no part of this book may be reproduced in any form or by any means, electronic or mechanical, including photocopying or recording, or by information storage or retrieval system, without permission in writing from the Publisher.

Published in the United States by Cleis Press Inc., P.O. Box 14697, San Francisco, California 94114.

Printed in the United States.
Cover design: Scott Idleman
Cover photograph: Leslie Lyons
Text design: Frank Wiedemann
Logo art: Juana Alicia
First Edition.
10 9 8 7 6 5 4 3 2 1

"Boogie Dykes" by Michelle Tea was originally published in the *San Francisco Bay Guardian,* Jan. 2001. "Hooker Booker" by K. St. Germaine originally appeared in *Tease* magazine no. 10, 2004. "In the Closet with Barbie" by Harlyn Aizley originally appeared on FreshYarn.com, Nov. 19, 2004. An earlier version of "Sex with Storm Troopers" by Annalee Newitz originally appeared on Salon.com, Sept. 2001. "Starfucker" by Paul Festa was originally published on Nerve.com; reprinted with permission, © 2005 Paul Festa and Nerve.com.

Library of Congress Cataloging-in-Publication Data

Best sex writing 2005 / edited by Violet Blue.— 1st ed.
    p. cm.
  ISBN 1-57344-217-8 (pbk. : alk. paper)
  1. Sex. I. Blue, Violet.
  HQ21.B617 2005
  306.7—dc22

                                        2005011386

Acknowledgements

Thanks go, first and foremost, to my publishers, Felice Newman and Frédérique Delacoste, for making this book possible.

I compiled these articles as a labor of love, and I want to especially thank the writers for understanding the idea that shaped the content—their experiences. Special thanks go to Robin Postell, who I think is one of the greatest unsung female sex journalists of our time. Jodi Wille from *Tease* magazine: thank you for everything; Rachel Kramer Bussel, I'm grateful especially for your suggestions and the offer of cupcakes. Extra-special thanks and smooches go to the cool websites and magazines that allowed the reprints of the material. Thanks and love go, as ever, to my personal support teams: my friends Carly Milne, Alison Tyler, Jonno D'Addario, Xeni Jardin, Chriso and Theresa Sparks; my family at Survival Research Laboratories—especially Mark Pauline; my family in the Extra Action Marching Band; and the man I love so very much, and who loves me back more than I can imagine, every single day—Courtney.

CONTENTS

Introduction: Things You Should Know
Violet Blue

There are things you should know. What is so familiar by day is inside-out at night. Strange and wondrous—and sometimes shocking—memories are being made between the thighs of those around you. If you could make an MRI of the sex life of the people you see every day, if you could look behind all the closed doors across America, what would you see?

The selections in *Best Sex Writing 2005,* which comprise recent writings both unpublished and previously published, show that American sex culture is not what you might think. This collection of essays is a veritable travel journal of the intersections of sex and people's lives, and it is entirely unpredictable. Every experience is true, and often shocking, and yet every experience is not uncommon.

These stories are daring, exciting, harsh, and relevant. They open a revealing window into the human condition, and into our sexuality as a culture. Our culture avoids direct eye contact with sex and sexuality; likely every "true story" you've read and seen on-screen qualifies the topic of sex by compulsively dressing it up as silly, rude, boring, offensive, scholarly, sensational, or spiritual. But the truth is, sex is so much more interesting when it's real, authentic, and presented passionately—without hidden messages of "good" and "bad"—which is precisely why I was compelled to collect these pieces into a book. The writing explosion ushered in by the blogosphere has created dialogue about sex like nothing we've ever seen, and has rendered sex-with-a-moral irrelevant, revealing naked truths and authentic insights into our sexual natures by way of real experiences. And it's about time. The stories here aren't candy-coated, nor are they boring essays—they're a thrill ride.

In "Sperm Bank Teller," for instance, Polly Enmity explains how she got a job at a sperm bank, and you'll be startled to hear what really goes on within the walls of a medical facility that pays men to masturbate. "Dick Check" by Chris Ohnesorge relates the experience of a man whose job at a gay sex club in New York requires him to inspect the penises of each man who walks in the door. "Hooker Booker" by K. St. Germaine takes us on a no-holds-barred journey into the world of a female hooker booker, a woman who books sex workers for their appointments, from high-rise to ghetto.

Each essay has its own riveting story to tell about a collision with sexual culture. In "Boogie Dykes," Michelle Tea crashes the very straight world of porn when she visits the Adult Video News Awards with a group of lesbian porn filmmakers. Patrick Califia delivers a piece that simply must be read through in one intense sitting in "Sex with the Imperfect Stranger," where in exploring a murder case, he delves into the reasons why someone would kill after sex. In "South Bronx, Sex Ed," Ellen Friedrichs relates the harrowing and heroic struggle to teach kids about sex and HIV in one of the toughest neighborhoods in the nation. "In the Closet with Barbie" by Harlyn Aizley tells a familiar story of a girl who plays with her dolls in ways surely not recommended by the manufacturer, revealing how many of us coped with the lack of accuracy we found beneath their tiny plastic belts.

Take a sex tour around the United States, and the unusual stories reveal astounding lives behind everyday façades. Timothy Archibald discovered exactly this when he traveled far and wide to meet the inventors behind a strange and large sexual subculture in "Sex Machines." Dr. Carol Queen takes a fascinating and unusual spiritual journey to the Kinsey Institute, complete with behind-the-scenes revelations, in "Visiting Kinsey." Sex and technology writer Annalee Newitz journeys to a place in America where time and space cease to exist—a sci-fi convention—and acts on urges we typically only keep to ourselves, in "Sex with Storm Troopers."

In two utterly compelling pieces, sex is experienced outside American culture, yet still seen through the lens of the American writer. Robin Postell takes us into the legendary "Boys Town" for an evening filled with danger, sex, and shocking acts in a Mexican town populated entirely by prostitutes. "Khajuraho" is Arlo Tolesco's private odyssey to the hidden, secret erotic temples of India, and the unique type of frustration they can inspire in a horny American abroad.

Each experience is illuminating, perfect, and poignant. Taken from the real-life online blog of a porn performer, "A Beginning: from 'God's Wife'" by Shirley Shave powerfully chronicles her intense entry into the world of onscreen sex for money. In "Superheroines in Trouble" Don Rasner opens a door into a highly unusual sexual subculture whose roots are steeped in an unsettling violence; the author admits that he's a consumer of the genre. Michael A. Gonzales visits "The Night Birds" and reports back from the front lines of paying for sex in New York. Carly Milne shows us in "My Porno Life" that being a nonperforming female in the Los Angeles pornography industry is like walking through a field studded with social, sexual, and sometimes even humorous land mines. Finally, Paul Festa's "Starfucker" manifests a cultural fantasy and viscerally transports us into modern mythological terrain, with a nice dose of oral sex thrown in for good measure.

I hope you enjoy taking these trips behind closed doors—and through plenty of open ones—as much as I have.

Violet Blue
San Francisco
June 2005

Boys Town: 200 Whores, 4 Classy Guys, and 1 Skinny Donkey
Robin Postell

We're dangling dangerously somewhere over San Antonio, Texas.

We'll land in Laredo, cross the border into Nuevo Laredo, Mexico, and pay a visit to Boys Town, also known as *La Zona*, or *Zona Rosa*—a teeming village of bawdy prostitutes. According to Andy, it's a tiny, thriving community where women walk around in their underwear hawking their wares for American dollars. Back in the '60s and '70s it was a soothing getaway for Vietnam vets. It's been renovated lately and still has quite an allure for those looking to score some cheap, no-nonsense ass.

We're a motley crew. MC for the night is Andy, who owns a handful of titty bars and nude tanning salons in the Dallas–Forth Worth area. He had a memorable but brief stint in the infamous Ultimate Fighting Championship's fifth installment but got his big opponent's thumb lodged in his eye, ending the match. Andy's rich, decadent, and from the wrong side of the tracks, which makes

1

for a well-rounded character. Completely insane, Andy relishes spending big bucks amazing his friends and acquaintances. This makes him a popular guy wherever he goes.

Lance, Andy's full-time pilot, is probably the sanest of us, which is some comfort. He refuses to drink before he flies and always tries to get his rest instead of staying up all night with everyone else. Up front with him is Doc, a Dallas physician with a penchant for the raunchy. I'm in the middle seats, sitting next to Andy, who wears a simple expression of ribald complacency.

In the back seat there's Tamale Joe, who invented a tamale-making machine. The bespectacled head resting on Tamale Joe's shoulder is Dragon Lee's, a taekwondo grandmaster from Korea who barely reaches five feet but can kill you with one chop of his calloused hands or feet.

Andy's telling me stories about Boys Town. He'd first told me about it at a fight in Kiev, Ukraine. I told him he was full of shit. He sent his pilot to pick me up to prove it to me.

"You've got to be kidding," I say to Andy, forever naïve.

"Really," he confirms. "Pussy for miles. Pussy as far as the eye can see."

We've landed in Laredo. As soon as we cross the border into Nuevo Laredo I smell raw sewage and tacos. The streets are grimy and sweaty, filth the norm. The heat makes you drunk, sticky, and slow. Cars and taxis ramble around with the windows rolled down, Latino beats blasting from cheap, busted speakers. Drunk tourists meander glassy-eyed. We look for a restaurant but it's too late. Andy hails a taxi and we pile in. It's a ten-dollar jaunt.

The taxi wings through Nuevo Laredo and passes a bullfighting arena teeming with bloodthirsty fans. Then it's upon us—the famed Boys Town, surrounded by a white concrete brick wall.

One way in, one way out. I study the garish, neon-embossed entrance with cars swarming in and out like worker bees to a hive. Everybody's car windows are down. You hear Mexican pop jams, laughter, drunken banter. It's a pumping fiesta, dusty as a spaghetti Western. Andy pays the cab driver as we peel our damp bodies off the vinyl car seats.

We stop off at a corner fajita stand just inside the entrance where short, perspiring Mexican men are cooking strips of flank steak on an outdoor grill thick with soot and grease. Andy makes some remark about its not being beef, to be funny.

We sit at one of the outdoor tables. I'm looking around for naked chicks.

"*Quatro Carta Blancas, por favor,*" Andy says to the sweaty waitress. Andy points across the dusty street to a dark building. "That's the clinic where all the girls get checked out," he explains.

Prostitution is legal in Mexico, but confined to these red zones like Boys Town. Guarded by lethargic *federales,* whose presence is prominent (some even somberly wagging machine guns at the entrance), Boys Town is an attempt to keep at least some of the deadly sins corralled in designated areas.

Apparently the women who hook here are required to get physical exams every week and carry a card resembling a passport with their photo and script stating they're healthy enough to bang. They receive these from the Boys Town physician, who works on-site at the clinic. In addition to their weekly exams, they have blood work done twice yearly, testing for HIV and hepatitis. Free condoms are given out, or can be purchased for a buck when you choose your chick du jour, and while if you ask the women whether they use them they always say yes, plenty of horny guys have paid double to toss the latex.

"Show me something," I say to my crew. They all nod at each

other and smile smugly, scarfing down the fajitas with verde sauce.

Doc and Tamale Joe are sprawled out in the wrought iron chairs at the Tamyko Club, smiles plastered on their mugs. They're looking around at the women who walk around in their underwear and stiletto heels. Tamale Joe wears a baseball cap with I LOVE TAMALES stenciled in red across the front. We're discussing the tamale-making machine, for which he says he's getting a lot of orders lately. He makes the machines by hand, so it takes him a while to get the orders out. Then he tells me that if I go stand by the jukebox, that means I'm available. I see a few chicks standing by it. Immediately I note that none of them would turn me on if I were a man. This disappoints me. I wanted to be surrounded by hot horny babes, not hot horny whores. What did I expect?

We're sitting at a table that has a huge column in the center that blocks everyone's view of everyone else except the person sitting directly to your left or right. It's an absurd bit of social engineering, so I choose to wander around instead of sit there craning my neck and straining my voice to make small talk with my posse. I excuse myself, Carta Blanca in hand, while the boys get doused.

On my way to the john I get a load of the place. When you exit the main lounge area there's a center court filled with greenery—big leafy trees and short, rubbery-leafed shrubs. Flowers in concrete urns squat next to weathered wrought iron tables and chairs scattered about the place. The court is surrounded by a fort of rooms for rent by the half hour. When you choose a girl she pays the bartender five bucks for a key. Prices are negotiable behind closed doors but usually it's between ten and a hundred dollars, averaging about forty-five. There are two levels, with black stairs jutting up them.

A heavy Mexican girl in a G-string teddy and high-heeled patent leather sandals leads a skinny, grinning American teenager up the stairs to the second floor. He takes short glances back to the ground level where his friends rib one another and giggle.

The ladies' room is a crack in the wall near the bar, no frills, just the essentials: a mirror and a commode. I smack my rose/gunmetal colored Chanel lips and return to the masses. A guy approaches me and says, "Hey, I need a girlfriend." He leans into me slightly and lays one hand on the trunk of a tree. "I'm not a hooker," I say, trying to enunciate so he'll get my drift. "I'm here with friends." His English is not so good and I never make up my mind whether he gets what I'm telling him, but it doesn't matter anyway. I ain't the one.

There's a group of Texas boys standing around in pinpoint ox-fords and brown leather loafers. They all look eighteen—which is Mexico's legal drinking age. They say they come here every other weekend, smoke a joint, and freak out on chicks. But they say they never buy one. There's a cherub-faced girl sitting on one of their laps and I ask her what it's like, to hook here. "It's work," she says in a thick accent. "It's not love."

I ask her how many times a week she has sex and she says, "How many times a week do *you* have sex?" She goes on to say, in Span-ish, which one of the teenagers translates for me, that she has only been working here thirty days and she hates it. But she is saving up money to go to medical school to become a doctor. She says many of the women here are saving their money to start businesses, like hair salons or clothing boutiques. Many of the women live here inside the compound, some with children, in tiny rooms, she says. You see these rooms, doors opened, with their lonely, needy occu-pants standing sweatily at the thresholds, hoping someone will come save them, maybe tote them across the border to greener pastures.

Andy's looking for me, thinking I'm getting raped and knifed out back. He meets me at the door. We sit at one of the tables in the courtyard and he hails the waitress. "*Dos Carta Blancas, por favor,*" he says. Andy waves over a group of loitering musicians. One has a small guitar, the other a huge bass, and another an accordion. Andy knows everyone and they eye him lovingly. Word is that Andy's penis is so enormous that one hooker gave him his money back. She's here tonight. I fully intend on pulling her over to the side and asking her about this, to settle yet another one of Andy's tall tales once and for all.

Soon the others have gotten wise to what's going on and join us in the center courtyard. A couple of hookers sit down with us, wearing nothing but clingy see-through lingerie and high heels.

It's getting looser. Everybody's milling about. The poor girls smell money. We're gradually collecting an entourage. After everyone polishes off their swill, we cut out for the next place. There are so many, you must move through them quickly—scan the premises while you drink a beer. If it looks good, stick around. If not, move on. Since this is Andy's way to prove he's not a bullshit artist, he wants to make sure I see as much as possible until his point is proven beyond a reasonable doubt. I'm already convinced.

The next stop, and the most famous bar in Boys Town, is the Papagayo Club. It is larger and more like a regular bar, with better-looking women. A big room with tables and chairs, threaded down one side with a bar. Chicks walk around in their panties and whatever other kind of foxy outfit they have fashioned out of little pieces of fabric. It's obvious these guys are familiar with the place because they recognize girls and talk about them as they pass. They've probably done them all. In fact, every now and then Doc will lean over and tell me if one swallows or not, or whether another likes it up the ass.

"You're a classy guy," I tell him.

★   ★   ★

There are thirty-eight bars in Boys Town and we've hit about four. I'm getting the hang of it. I can't help but wonder whether these girls are having a good time. They look like they are. But I know the ways of women. They can fake a lot of things—orgasms being only one.

We've got a big round table and the women are swarming around. Even though the women usually work one bar, many have traveled from other clubs because they've heard about the rich titty-club owner and his drunk pals. None of my crew has hooked up with any women yet. I was expecting them to be in and out of rooms with a different hooker every half hour. But I always overestimate the appetites of men.

Doc and Tamale Joe are being picky. This one's too fat, the other one's nose is too big. Another has a pimple. I'm officially in charge of picking out women for them because I have declared I have better taste in women than they do.

Dragon Lee has never seen anything like this before, and it shows, but he is hanging in there. Earlier in the day he was doing a tae kwon do exhibition at a big tournament with kiddies wearing yellow belts in a Christian school gymnasium. I saw him chop three concrete blocks in two with one hand, then slice off cleanly the neck of a Jack Daniels bottle, barely spilling a drop or upsetting the bottle in the least. Tonight he's slamming tequila and tweaking the titties of whores whom he's bouncing on his knee. Andy waves over a couple of *damas* and they sit down, one on either side of Dragon Lee. Fifty bucks is passed into the thinner one's hand. Andy nods at Dragon Lee and whispers something in his ear. The young Mexican girl in the black thong bikini takes him by the hand and leads him away.

Then I see the girl of my dreams. No other woman in Boys

Town compares. She is tall and thin for a Mexican, with warm, moist dark skin and long sultry legs. She's wearing a black G-string and a black bra, her tits spilling over. If I were a guy, this is the one I'd do. I nudge Doc and nod at her. "Go get her," he says. "I'll take her."

I run off into the crowd after her, trailing her, listening to her stiletto heels click on the dirty stone floor. She senses me behind her and turns. Our eyes meet. I ask her to join us and she takes my hand. "You're beautiful," she says.

We sit down at our table, our bare thighs brushing against each other. When she talks to me, she touches my knee for emphasis and her fingertips linger. I'm pissed that Doc's going to take her and violate her, but she says she's got a kid at home she's got to feed. "It is necessary," she says in broken English when I tell her she doesn't have to go off with Doc if she doesn't want to. Her name is Aurora and she is so beautiful and sad I give her my diamond bracelet. This is how men get taken, I think.

Andy has ordered tequila shots for everyone and she's getting drunk. She leans over and asks me if I want to do some cocaine. She wobbles off unsteadily to get her purse and then returns, guiding me into the bathroom. Off the end of her long red fingernail I snort a couple of bumps and she kisses me before we go back out. Neither one of us is drunk anymore and she's got enough guts to go give Doc the fifty-dollar blow job he's been waiting for. Something about this bothers me but I deal with it. Mexican women here are poor. The unemployment rate is so high in Mexico that when jobs do become available only the men get lucky. At least she's making money, buying shoes for the baby. I tell Andy I want to take her back to Texas and put her up in an apartment, take care of her. "*I* will," he says. "You know I will if you want me to."

He would. He has so many whores put up in Texas apartments,

his accountant sweats himself to sleep nightly trying to finagle the books.

We leave Papagayo with Andy fuming. I sidle up next to him to get the scoop. Dragon Lee took the girl Andy bought for him and then left her lying on the bed because she had an ugly C-section scar. Doc's going to catch up later—he's off doing God-only-knows-what to Aurora. Tamale Joe is smacking his lips because he got lucky with a tiny hooker from Cozumel. Andy's being good, strangely, keeping me company, abstaining from the reindeer games. Every hooker in the joint lavishes attention on him, but he holds court stolidly.

We have still only been in a handful of bars and Andy is determined to show me the meat and bones of the place—saving the best for last. We skip Monkey's, which has a big fake gorilla standing out front. Andy tells me a guy is dressed up in a gorilla suit and has sex with a woman. The show's not that great, Andy says, rolling his eyes. There are sex shows aplenty here, most of them themed. Lesbians, heteros, monkeys.

And donkeys.

He saves the best for last. Marta's. A donkey, a real one, is tied up suspiciously outside the entrance and a wiry Mexican man is screaming at passersby to come watch the show. The donkey doesn't look happy, ribs protruding. "Why feed him when he's got all the pussy he can stand?" Andy laughs.

"Human pussy, at that," cries a drunk Tamale Joe.

The ASPCA would have a field day here.

Inside we grab a booth and Andy orders a round of Carta Blancas and shots of tequila. Women of all ages and descriptions mingle about the darkened, low-roofed space. Elaborate makeup and costumes abound. The walls are covered in red foil, which lends the decor a hellish flair. Diamond-shaped smoked mirrors are hung haphazardly on the walls. A glowing jukebox squats in the rear. Wobbly tables and vinyl booths surround a central dance floor. A mariachi band of fat, wet men in dirty clothes grinds out tunes. Perched on a wooden two-by-four shelf over our table is a huge black-eyed owl that drinks water from half of a plastic milk jug. Free to do as it pleases, it occasionally takes flight for the other side of the bar.

About this time Doc saunters in, the snake. "She swallowed every drop," he whispers into my ear proudly. I want to punch him.

By this time we've accumulated quite a following of personable hookers who all know Andy, Doc, and Tamale Joe by name and penis size. One of the hookers, Christiani, tells me that ninety percent of the "women" in this bar are really *hombres*. She says they work here to save up money for their operations. Most of the "girls" have ass and breast implants and take hormones as well. This sheds new light on the situation. I squint, searching for the tell-tale signs of manhood, but it's almost impossible to detect anything.

"Where are their dicks?" I ask Christiani. She tells me they tie a string around the head and pull it back between their asscheeks, where they secure it with tape.

A dancer in a black G-string slithers over to our table and Doc says, "Can you believe that's a man?" I can't. Her name is Deana and she has braces. Her tits aren't big but she does indeed have tits and they don't look fake and damn sure don't look manly.

She speaks no English and seems to be much more secure with her body than any of the females in the compound. In fact, all the tranny women here at Marta's seem more at ease and happier than the women. Deana sits between Doc and me and downs a shot of tequila. I'm feeling her breasts, trying to detect a silicone bag, but it's difficult. The skin is tight but not unnaturally so. More like the taut skin of a teenager. I try to look for an Adam's apple but she keeps moving and I don't want to be too obvious.

Deana gets up on our table and starts taking off her clothes and I'm sure any minute I'm going to see a penis and testicles drop between her smooth, solid thighs. She's careful, though. Something in the way she moves makes me think she's hiding something—something about the linear quality of her pelvis. Dragon Lee is looking for a penis, too, now that he's been cued in. Neither one of us believes she's a guy. After a few more shots of tequila, no one cares. They squeeze lime juice on her chest and tell me to lick it off, and I do.

The mariachi band takes a break and a Muzak version of John Lennon's "Imagine" sets a new mood. There's a commotion at the entrance as the lights dim. The small club is filling with patrons. An overweight dancer makes her way out into the center of the dance floor holding a banana. The woes of too many babies are clearly defined on her saggy abdomen. Andy locks his eyes on mine and nods, in-the-know. In seconds she's peeled the banana and is on her back. To everyone's surprise, demure Dragon Lee takes half of it and squats down beside the supine woman, sticking it in her holiest of holies. Andy, meanwhile, won't take his eyes off me and can't stop laughing. There is something demonic about Andy, perhaps because his father is an infamous televangelist in Texas.

Two tired, old *señors* lead in the equally tired, old donkey. One man stands in front, the other in the rear, and with some shuffling dexterity they grab the poor burro's legs and topple him over on his prickly back. This is disturbing and ridiculous to observe, but more so when the banana lady straddles him. I watch the woman grinding on the overturned beast and think about how my Mama would be shaking her head. *If they could see me now, that little gang of mine....*

A tranny with a wild Farrah Fawcett mane sits next to me. She's sporting a long sequined gown, the neckline diving in between two smallish breasts. She's up next.

Christiani is laughing, licking salt off Andy's exposed neck and downing another shot of tequila. I get her attention.

"Did you really give Andy his money back because his dick's so big?" I ask.

"Yes," she smiles, nuzzling him. "I did."

"What'd you think about the donkey show?" Andy asks me.

"I think you're a classy guy," I chuckle, down a shot of tequila, and watch the transvestites convince Doc it really doesn't matter that they used to be guys.

The Night Birds
Michael A. Gonzales

"You've got to explore what is taboo in you…"
—Macy Gray,
"Sexual Revolution"

It was past midnight, and I had been instructed by the raspy-voiced receptionist from Hot-N-Tot Escorts, a service that specialized in "thick black chicks," to check in from the pay phone on the corner of 50th Street and 8th Avenue. Folding the paper, I studied the photos of the trio of girls in the back of the *Village Voice* before making a final selection. Godiva was bent over in a sheer teddy that held no secrets, her russet rump spilling out of her lingerie and her thick thighs promising a thunderous good time.

During the daylight hours, 50th Street bustled with screaming schoolkids, motley messengers, well-dressed women, and sharp-suited businessmen. Yet, on that breezy Monday in November, with the exception of an occasional speeding taxi, the sidewalk was desolate. Dropping two quarters into the phone slot, I tensely scanned the numerous neighborhood windows while dialing the printed number.

"Hot-N-Tot," answered the smoky-voiced girl.

"Hey," I muttered. "I'm the guy who had the one o'clock appointment with Godiva."

"You know it's one-fifty, right?" the smoldering voice asked. I felt the crisp roll of twenties inside my khaki pants pocket. "Just walk to the Days Hotel a block away, go through the lobby and up to the fourth floor. Godiva will meet you in the hallway."

Peering into the darkness, I saw a flock of pigeons roosting on a ledge across the street. "No problem," I said, hanging up the receiver.

I ambled through the well-lit lobby of the hotel. Staring into the mirror beside the elevator, I wondered who I'd call if I was busted by an undercover sting operation targeting escort girls; would the next day's cover of the *New York Post* feature my scared face?

Once the elevator doors swooshed open and I saw the crooked smile of the cocoa-hued Godiva, all apprehension melted away. From the texture of her skin it was obvious Godiva had chosen her moniker from the expensive chocolates, not that naked babe on the horse. Dressed in a black Baby Phat sweat suit, Godiva asked, "You're not a cop, are you?"

"No. Are you?" Shaking her bone-straight weave, Godiva tenderly grabbed my shirtsleeve and led me into an unheated hotel room. Nervously, I looked around. There was a scarred night table and a floral-patterned spread on the bed. Underfoot, the stained carpet was in desperate need of a shampoo.

"Is this your first time?" Godiva asked sweetly. She grinned when I nodded. "Don't worry...everything will be fine." Picking up a brown Gucci travel bag, she kissed me on the cheek. "Just make yourself comfortable while I go change." Watching her stroll into the small bathroom, I pulled a hydro blunt out of my wallet as Mos Def 's "Ms. Fat Booty" spun on the turntable in my mind.

While Godiva was gone, I remembered the first time I fell in love with the whores of New York. Waddling through sleazy Times Square in the late 1970s, I was enthralled by the circus of lights, shrill verbal fights, and half-naked flesh erupting on the block. A slow-moving kid dressed in husky-sized jeans and Pro-Keds, I found my young eyes straying toward a flock of fiercely styled sisters strutting down the sidewalk. Stopping, the rainbow-hued crew of vulgar ladies lurked in front of an arcade doorway.

Over the game room soundtrack of pinball machines and Space Invaders, the women applied a fresh coat of makeup. Clad in high-heeled boots, low-cut dresses, and cheap jewelry, they were unlike any girls I had ever seen. Immediately, I was attracted to the scorching heat of their bad-girl flames.

Truth be told, at the time I wasn't even aware of their profession. Surrounded protectively by Catholic school nuns, Boy Scout den mothers, and conservative parents, I surely found the hookers' subterranean universe beyond my prepubescent understanding.

It wasn't until later that I discovered a ragged newspaper in the Shalimar Barbershop that changed my life. Rummaging through the splintered window seat stacked with old issues of *Sepia, Jet,* and *Ebony*, I abruptly stopped when a hedonistic spirit blessed me with a crinkled newspaper called *Screw*.

Founded by Al Goldstein in the days before weekly alternative newspapers like the *Village Voice* made much bank running ads for call-girl services and local brothels, *Screw* was a pioneering tabloid of sex in the city. Gazing at the illustrated cover of a full-busted cartoon babe (perhaps drawn by former *Mad* magazine genius

Wally Wood) who flashed Vanessa Del Rio lips, I felt delirious.

With phone numbers listed below the women's provocative photographs, I found it difficult to fathom that there was an entire sexual landscape hidden behind the gleaming skyscrapers of the city.

Without even trying, right there in the barbershop I had discovered a sexual wonderland of raven-haired *señoritas*, blonde dominatrixes, and brown-skinned beauties. Unlike the lessons I had learned in the hallowed classrooms at St. Catherine of Genoa, I realized that sex wasn't just about eternal promises of fidelity. Looking at the images of naked women, I was overcome with a feeling of perverted liberation that went beyond the pages of any girlie magazine.

As I found out later, unlike the airbrushed, ivory-skinned bunnies posing in *Playboy*, the women in *Screw* were real girls who were attainable...for a small fee.

After glancing at those sordid snapshots, the soft flesh of hard women was forever etched on my mind.

But that was long ago. Now, an atomic marijuana cloud was hovering over the room as Godiva slinked out of the bathroom to join me. Scantily dressed in a light pink leather miniskirt with matching spaghetti-strapped shoes and halter top, she fluttered her fake eyelashes like a Chinese fan.

"You can do whatever you want, except fuck me in the ass or kiss me on the mouth," she said. "Oh, and I need to get the money up front."

Having been celibate for three months, I was anxious. "It's cold in here," I replied. "Lets get under the covers." Keeping her heels on, Godiva climbed under the bedclothes. Although I hadn't noticed her placing a rubber into her mouth, when Godiva pulled off my Hilfiger underwear and placed her thick lips around my cock, the lubricated condom was in place.

Seductively removing her halter, Godiva rubbed her hardened nipples against my bearded face. I stuck two fingers into her hon-eyed moistness, to find her woolly pubic hair as soft as cashmere.

"I'd rather be eaten than fingered," she whispered. Under the influence of her professional passion, the next thirty-five minutes of my life was a period of exquisite savagery. Indeed, as I sucked her bulging breasts and licked sweat from her soft belly, I felt a hallucinatory dualism of heated fervor and cold detachment. As a former romantic who once believed in the lie of love, I felt a sensuous guilt released with each of Godiva's graceful movements and my brutal grunts.

"Is it good?" she whispered, her hefty body leaning to the side of the bed.

"Yes," I moaned. As exhilarated pleasure and shame surged through me, one last thrust brought me closer to rapture.

Afterward, Godiva and I lay sweating in the bed and held each other as though I had just given her my class ring. Lying in the darkness with a satisfied smile on my face, I felt as though I had been baptized in the river Styx.

For, after years of perpetuating the role of the good boy that I was raised to be, in her arms I felt empowered by our sinful deed. At the precise moment that most sane men were in their homes snoring next to their wives or girlfriends, I was crazily content be-ing anonymous with a call-girl in a crummy hotel room.

"You were trying to fuck the shit out of me," Godiva said with a laugh, snapping me out of my reverie.

"It's been a long time," I answered, stroking her smooth bot-tom. Propping up the pillow, I reached over to the night table for the remainder of the reefer. Taking a toke, I offered the blunt to Godiva.

"Naw, it's cool," she said. "I might have to take a drug test next week." Reaching into the travel bag, she retrieved a crumpled pack of Newports.

"Dig that," I answered. "What's the test for? You trying to get a new job?" Although I didn't intend to sound sarcastically superior, it came out that way.

"Naw, nothing like that. I had some problems last year and my bitch mother has custody of my son. For me to visit, I have to be clean. I never know when I might get my piss tested."

"How old is your kid?"

Leaning on her elbow, Godiva smiled. "He's three going on forty-three," she said. "His name is DeVante. He was conceived while I was listening to a Jodeci record."

"Understood. So, what happened?"

Sucking her cigarette-stained teeth, Godiva replied, "I got busted last year when I was working in a spot uptown. Somebody snitched, and next thing I know five-oh knocked down the door. It wasn't the first time I got busted, so I did a few months upstate. I asked my mother to watch the baby, but when I got out she refused to give DeVante back. The bitch went to court, and the whole nine."

"Maybe the kid is better off," I said, and immediately knew I had made a mistake. "I mean...."

"I know what you mean," she snapped. Four stories below, a siren screamed in the night. Godiva reached for her halter and stood up. After tying the top, she looked at her thin silver watch and said, "I have another customer coming in twenty minutes."

Dressing quickly, I felt like an asshole. Godiva politely opened the door. As I turned to walk down the hallway, she screamed, "Just because I'm a ho doesn't mean I'm a bad mother, you know." A few doors down from the hotel, I entered an all-night French bistro called Pigalle. Soft saxophone sounds streamed from the speakers. A raven-haired Argentine waiter took my order. Moments later, nursing a dirty Amidalle martini, I relived the prior hour in my mind as though it were an urban noir film with a lush Marvin Gaye score.

Ever since my experience a young kid in the Shalimar Barbershop, I've been enticed by the ways of whores. As a teenager living in Baltimore, I spent many nights roaming with my homeboy, Ronny, around the red-light district known as The Block. Popping into spots with names like The Two O'Clock Club and Bottom's Up, we drank illegally and watched the seductive dance of stiletto-heeled strippers. Dressed in baby-doll nighties, the girls gyrated to soulful grooves blaring from the DJ booth.

Over the years, although I've spent innumerable dollar bills at strip clubs, the idea of paying for sex had always seemed somewhat distasteful. Who were these desperate men known as tricks, and why couldn't they simply find their kicks at home instead of embracing strangers in the night?

While one could argue that the countless lap dances, ass slaps, and garter snaps might be perceived as sexual, since there was no penetration, I've always thought otherwise.

Of course, since that time I've had my share of casual lovers and serious relationships, but nothing had a sense of danger as that one transient liaison with Godiva. And, like any other kind of junkie, I simply wanted more.

Two weeks later, chilling in my book-cluttered room, continuously listening to Me'Shell Ndegeocello's melancholy masterpiece "Bitter," I decided to visit the nest of another nocturnal creature. Flipping through the *Village Voice*, this time I called Lush Ladies for an appointment. Lush Ladies was an in-call spot, which was a modern way of saying *brothel;* the building's neighbors, I later learned, were paid off so they wouldn't complain about the traffic of single men. I made an appointment for nine that night, and took a steaming shower before venturing into the evening.

Ironically located around the corner from an ex-girlfriend's apartment, the Lush Ladies pad was a medium-sized residence in the east 20s—an upwardly mobile neighborhood filled with ivory-skinned yuppies straight out of a Jay McInerney novel.

I was met at the door by a buxom white chick named Savannah, who inquired in a southern accent if I was a cop. As an added precaution, she frisked me thoroughly. As she guided me through the spacious apartment into a bedroom, I heard the blissful moans of a satisfied customer from behind a closed door. "Take off your clothes and I'll be right back," Savannah said.

Not being into white women, I rudely asked, "Do I get a choice?" Walking out the door, Savannah snickered.

The room contained a framed psychedelic pop-art poster painted by Peter Max: a silhouette of a woman's angular face, with the word LOVE boldly painted in blue letters. Stripping down to my boxer shorts, I sat in a black leather La-Z-Boy next to the full-sized bed.

In a matter of minutes, Savannah returned. As if in a modern-day slave auction, she bought in five black *flye* females. She introduced each negligee-clad chick by her given moniker (Fire, Dream, and so on), and each one politely said, "Hello." Overwhelmed, I quickly chose an Amazonian, red-boned babe with almond eyes named China. She wore silver-hooped earrings and her thick black hair flowed to her broad shoulders.

With disappointment, the other four women filed out of the room.

China was a curvy chick who couldn't have been much older than nineteen. Although she had the thickness, her body was tight and her skin was the color of butterscotch. When she spoke, I could see her silver tongue ring. With thick, smooth legs and an ample ass, China wore a crimson-colored teddy with matching heels that strapped around the ankles.

China lit a cinnamon-scented candle on the dresser and dimmed the lights. Lounging across the bed, she asked, "So why did you pick *me?*" For such a gorgeous girl, her voice sounded insecure.

"Well," I replied, and sat next to her. China smelled as though she had taken a bath in rose petals. "Well, I thought you were the most attractive."

"Really?" China beamed. Although I detected a slight accent, I couldn't pinpoint where she was from. "Are you for real?" From a neighboring room one of the girls blasted "The Miseducation of Lauryn Hill." The luminous music seeped through the walls.

"Yeah," I answered, and chuckled. "When I first got here I thought I was stuck with the white chick."

"Don't laugh," China scolded playfully. "Savannah makes more money here than any of us."

"You serious?"

"As a heart attack," China said. "A lot of black dudes come here for her. Mostly older guys, but a few young ones too."

"Who would have thought?"

"Yeah," China replied. "It's kind of messed-up, 'cause if she ain't here, they don't even want to fuck none of the black girls. They just leave. But, I heard she gets down pretty good."

"Where you from?"

"Oakland. Been here a few months. My mom is Korean."

"Word. That's some funny shit. If your mom is Korean, why do you call yourself China?"

"I don't know," she said. "I used to get teased a lot in school 'cause I was half Korean. I beat up a guy in high school once when he called me a 'black chink.'"

"So you thought being Chinese was better?"

"Not better, just different." I began rubbing her silky pubic area, my thumb massaging her corpulent clit. "So what are you looking for?" China asked, licking her full lips.

"Looking for...?" I asked. "What you mean?"

"I mean, you want a golden shower or a brown shower or...."

"A brown shower," I said, stifling a laugh. "You mean people pay you to shit on them."

"Some people, yeah."

"Naw, that's too freak nasty for a nigga like me. How about just regular sex. Or is that extra?"

She pulled the teddy over her head and tossed it on the floor. China smiled, and opened her fleshy legs and I went down on her. From the next room I heard fingers snapping, and then realized it was Lauryn and D'Angelo's "Nothing Really Matters." She moaned as I gently licked her sweetness.

After I came up for air, China stretched an arm out. Reaching under the pillow, she pulled out a condom. With slender fingers, China slipped the rubber onto me. Before moving her hand, she brought my prick into her searing mouth. Thrillingly, I felt the stud of her tongue ring along the shaft.

"Bend over," I whispered. As the bedroom seemed to drift out to sea, I looked at China's ass and grinned. For the next half-hour, the world was a beautiful place. After I came, we lay in a heap on the crinkled sheets. China had a pained expression on her face. "What's wrong?" I asked.

"Nothing," she lied. I looked at my watch. There were ten minutes left to my hour.

Rubbing her full breasts, I leaned over and gently kissed her belly. Suddenly, I heard a knock on the bedroom door. "Time's up!" Savannah shouted.

For the next few days I thought about China whenever I walked into a Korean deli, heard Lauryn Hill on the radio, or spotted wrapped butterscotch in the candy shop. After borrowing $150 from my homeboy, Jerry (I lied and said I needed it for rent), I called Lush Ladies Escorts again.

"China's not working today," the receptionist said.

"Damn. What about tomorrow? Is she working tomorrow?"

"Well, to tell the truth, China quit. She doesn't work here anymore. I think she went back to California." I felt a ping in my heart. How could I have fallen in love with a girl I didn't even know, a girl whose job it was to make lonely hearts like mine feel special, if only for the hour? "Is there another girl you'd like to make an appointment with?"

For a moment I was silent. If, as I had reasoned, nothing seemed to matter more than my selfish dedication to the pursuit of decadent desires, I might as well try as many types of women as possible. Before I knew it, the image of a pretty white woman in black lace panties popped into my head.

During those intimate moments when I've been between a whore's warm legs, absorbing the bouquet of her perfume mixed with sweat, I've felt that the ugly reasons behind life's beautiful facade have had little meaning. In this straight-up world of ho's and tricks, lustful desires and a simple exchange of currency was all that mattered.

"Is Savannah working tonight?" I asked.

In the Closet with Barbie

Harlyn Aizley

The players: Barbie and Ken; a GI Joe whose muscular body twisted and bent in all the right places; a Cowboy whose hair and handsome cowboy outfit were both eerily a part of his body, plastic reliefs painted varying shades of brown; a "Julia" doll, the only doll of color—aside from Asian GI Joe—and the only health care worker; a small girl whose hair I cut short and declared "he" or "she" as the spirit moved me. What I did was sit in the closet and make them all have sex—not just casual flings, but heated dramas continuing from one day to the next, involving passionate triangles and tales of romantic tragedy, unrequited love, illicit sex, homosexuality, heterosexuality, reversible transsexualism. Objects from the dolls' dowries—a plastic horse, a small nurse's kit, a feather boa, a tiny replica of a World War II machete—I easily incorporated into my play as, eventually, I did with other objects not so readily available. The funny thing is, in the beginning it wasn't even sex that I was after; it was a penis. The sex just followed, as it usually does, once a penis is located.

I blame it on my conservative father and the fact that I have no brothers, that I didn't know what a penis looked like until well into my teens, late teens. L-a-t-e. As a preteen, I asked my mother to buy me boy dolls, thinking that I might get to see a penis. And so I lay further blame on Mattel, and on our repressed puritanical culture that refuses to make dolls anatomically correct to satisfy my need to sexualize every doll I ever owned.

Despite my ignorance, I had the evolutionary wherewithal to guess that, whatever the details, penises most likely were more substantial than the slight lumps Ken and GI Joe sported—the cowboy's anatomy obviously remained a mystery, sealed as it was beneath his permanent plastic clothing. If you want to see a penis, and you want your dolls to be able to have sex—real sex, not lump-mashing sex—then lumps are frustrating and entirely inadequate. I longed for the facts, the secret to which all the boys around me (and most of the girls) were privy. But mostly I longed for bulges. I wanted my male dolls to bulge obviously and firmly at the crotch. I wanted to be able to pull down their pants and find something there, taking up space, an explanation for why boys' underwear was different from my own. I wanted to see one, dammit. And later in life I wanted to *have* one, but that's a whole other story.

My younger sister, Carrie, saw a penis years before I did. In fact, the penis Carrie saw belonged to none other than our father. One summer our family spent a week in a small and smelly two-room cottage on Cape Cod. We all shared the bedroom, my parents on twin beds and Carrie and I on cots. One afternoon Carrie in-nocently came in from the beach looking for a towel. She padded into the bedroom without knocking and immediately was witness to my father changing into his bathing suit. He barked something at her and then chased the stunned but smiling six-year-old out of the room.

As soon as Carrie had regained her composure, she ran down the beach to where I was playing, and chanted, "I saw Daddy naked! I saw Daddy naked!"

Like any older sibling used to the painstaking measures each parent takes to maintain a semblance of equality between offspring—cutting perfectly symmetrical pieces of cake, spending exactly the same amount of money on birthday presents—I ran inside to claim what I had no doubt was rightly my due, a chance to see my father naked.

"I get to see him too," I announced to my mother who stood guard by the bedroom door.

"No, you don't." I know now that this was one of those pivotal parenting moments. "Go back outside while your father changes," the sentry said.

"But Carrie got to see him."

"Your sister walked into the bedroom by accident."

"Well, then I can too," I said as I tried to storm by my mother to reenact the incredible occasion. As if my father still was standing there, midchange, frozen in time until justice was served and balance restored to our eternally symmetrical family.

"It's not fair!" I shouted as my mother physically restrained me. I had wanted to see a penis for so long. And to make matters even more unbearable, as far as I knew, Carrie hadn't even wanted to see one. Besides, hadn't Carrie's faux pas broken the ice surrounding the issue of Dad's nudity? Like what difference would it make if another daughter saw him? Come on, the modesty gig is up, show me the goods.

Instead, my father came barreling out of the bedroom embarrassed and angry—not to mention dressed—and bellowed, "Outside! Now!" And that was that.

On the other hand, I was very well versed in the anatomy of women and girls. I knew that girls had either bald or blonde-haired vaginas and that when you grew up they grew curly dark hairs in the shape of a big triangle. (This hair color myth wasn't shattered until one day in the locker room at summer camp when I saw that my friend Janice, exactly my age, had dark down in her pubic region, the same color as my mother's curly triangle; revelation! The color of pubic hair has nothing to do with age.) I had seen the *Playboy* magazines owned secretly by the boys in the neighborhood, not to mention those owned secretly by my repressed, conservative father. My mother had even showered and taken baths with us when we were very young. So I knew, too, all about breasts and nipples, as well as their varying shapes and sizes.

Maybe it was because I was competent with female anatomy that I didn't feel as frustrated by the lack of detail among my female dolls. So none of them had nipples, big deal. It made me feel superior, as if I was more knowledgeable than the doll manufacturers. Every so often I would draw on a pair of nipples with a Magic Marker, but really it was hardly an issue.

The penis/lump thing, however, gnawed at me. Sex between my dolls became unsatisfying. Because, despite never having seen a penis, I did know a little bit about sex. My brazen mother, early on, unhesitatingly had answered the "where do babies come from/why do boys have penises/what is sex?" question with this informative story: A man and a woman love each other very much, and then the man puts his penis in the woman's vagina. She even bought me a book with some vague sketches of naked boys and girls asking their naked parents (!) similar questions, to which they received the same answer.

My best friend, Lori, who had an older brother and knew everything, confirmed this story, and once, to my extreme titillation, even acted it out for me. At any rate, the vague sketches revealed that boys had little hot-dogs instead of lumps. This made much more sense to me since I was a veritable expert on female genitalia and reasoned, therefore, that a lump could not possibly go into a vagina, thank you very much, while a hot dog could.

So the male-doll/lump frustration weighed heavily on me until one day, during a particularly steamy orgy in the closet, I was host to yet another revelation: Why not make penises and attach them to the guys? The idea excited me more than I care to admit. Enter: modeling clay. I burst out of the closet and began sculpting away. The results were remarkable. Ken now had a modest package beneath his dress pants. GI Joe had a nice bulge to match his biceps and washboard stomach. Even the transsexual packed a load. (If I was thrilled, one can only guess how Barbie and Julia felt, to say nothing of the small ballerina, who smelled like perfume.)

Since doll-sex took place in the closet, it's obvious that I already had internalized my parent's inclination to keep silent all evidence of sex or nudity. But now, unless I wanted to load and unload genitalia daily, all my doll-play would have to be relegated to the closet. I deemed it a small price to pay, and began a ritual of hiding my dolls and all their belongings in a box in the back corner of my bedroom closet. I couldn't figure out which would be worse—my parents finding out that my dolls were sexually active, or their discovering that I had carefully sculpted little clay penises and attached them to all the men.

Everything was going along fine. The cowboy, in his permanent plastic clothing, had had affairs with both the transsexual and Julia. Ken was gay most of the time. Barbie hung out with GI Joe, a lot. And I was quite content, having satisfied my desire for a well-hung cast of plastic friends. My sculptures even evolved a bit as I learned more about the anatomy of a penis (one day, Joey, a friend and neighbor, had sat cross-legged in his bathing suit offering me a quick glimpse of the bounty within).

So, given how well my clandestine doll-playing was going, I naturally got a bit lax in my secrecy. One day, just once, I left the doll box next to my bed rather than in the closet. One time only. Just one false move. My fatal flaw. I was downstairs watching television when Carrie, four feet tall, with crazy blonde hair and a small pot belly poking out from under her pink T-shirt, came into the den. She stared at me. A blonde, beer-drinking elf, staring at me with an expression akin to that of Perry Mason having just led his opponent into confessing the most heinous of crimes. Her eyes were on fire.

"You put clay down your dolls' pants," she said, grinning from ear to ear, as it was apparent she had just scored the most powerful of all weapons against me. Even potentially more dangerous than when she was told that I had to go see a "talking doctor" because I cried whenever my mother left me at my friend Wendy's house. They said I had separation anxiety but I think it was because Wendy's mother had a German accent and my post–World War II Jewish parents had taught me to fear all things German. Anyway, this was better. Because everyone on the block knew what dolls were. And everyone knew what clay was. And everyone knew that you don't put clay down your dolls' pants unless you were obsessed with shit or, God forbid, genitalia.

"You put clay down your dolls' pants," Carrie repeated, as she continued to stare at me. Proof that yes, in fact, her older sister truly was the most embarrassing creature who ever lived.

"Why did you put clay down your dolls' pants?" She was eight. I was eleven.

"Because."

Not interested in, or perhaps terrified of, the answer I might give, Carrie took off down the hall yelling, "Harlie puts clay down her dolls' pants. Harlie puts clay down her dolls' pants!" All around the house.

You'd think she would have raced into the street right then and there, to tell anyone she could find. But she didn't. She saved it. Saved it and tortured me with it. Blackmailed me as only an eight-year-old sister can. Threatened me with it whenever it suited her. Used it to get all sorts of things out of me. It worked better than when she turned up her lip and threatened to burst into tears if I wouldn't let her have a toy, the last cookie, whatever she desired at the moment.

Carrie saved it and played it for all it was worth. Until one day her moment came. She had been angry with me for I don't remember what—having taken the front seat in the car, having changed the channel, having gotten to stay up later than her too many nights in a row. I was sitting in my bedroom looking at magazines, not with Lori, my best friend, who somehow would have helped me to turn the tables on Carrie, but with Jamie and Renee, representatives of the "popular crowd." Sure, we were reading magazines, but we also were participating in some serious hazing. We were sixth-graders, rulers of the elementary school. Jamie and Renee were our two leaders. They were checking me out for potential inclusion in their clique.

Carrie, fuming at me, peeked her intuitive blonde head into my room. She waited until we all noticed her. And then she threw the grenade, "Harlie puts clay down her dolls' pants!"

There was silence for a moment. Terrible, dreadful, prepubescent silence during which an awful heat crept up my spine and into my face, causing me to blush the most embarrassing shade of red ever to be found in a New Jersey suburb. Even Carrie stood speechless and spent in the doorway, as unsure as I about what might happen next.

And then I got it. I would tell them it was a project for art class. While everyone else was told to go home and cut pictures out of magazines to make collages, I—because I knew so much about the anatomy of boys and men—was given special permission to sculpt genitalia out of clay. My little sister was just bragging.

But before I had a chance to gather my breath and spin my lie, Jamie and Renee, with looks that were a mixture of disdain and pity, said to me almost in unison, "You still play with dolls?"

Much to my surprise, their absolute inability to imagine the possibility of making clay penises and forcing your dolls to fuck their brains out somehow, suddenly made me the expert in male genitalia I'd always wanted to be. "Yeah," I said.

"That's cool."

"Whatever."

Carrie and I exchanged glances, and then she wandered away down the hall.

A Beginning: from "God's Wife"
Shirley Shave

Call me asshole. Two years ago today I answered an ad in the *Hollywood Press* for "Models wanted. No experience necessary. Call Monday thru Friday 12–7." Next to the ad was a photo of a woman in lingerie with a finger to her lips, as if keeping a secret. I was very low on money at the time. When I say low I mean I had none, my last dollar from a string of mind-numbing and, in some cases, hurtful waitressing jobs having gone to rent. I didn't even have enough money left for one meal. Rent always came first. I could live hungry, but I never wanted to live on the streets in the rain.

I was at a particularly low point in my life. Straight moms and dads and politicians and even rednecks might say that I was even lower now. Low—I mean so low that your feet burned because your were so close to Hell—was being raped by your boss during a stint waiting tables at the Sizzler while out front families scarfed down their ten-dollar all-you-can-eat shrimp. My boss raped me and then denied me a raise. On my best day I never took in more than thirty-five dollars. Everybody has to work, and most jobs are dull and insulting to the mind and don't pay any money. I am an educated person but that didn't seem to get me anywhere. So I swallowed the butterflies in my stomach and dialed the number in the ad.

A man named Bernard answered the phone and set up the interview for a Tuesday morning in his small office. When I got there, I found he was a large, muscled man with a thin beard. He had kind blue eyes, but a voice that bellowed even when whispering.

"You know, this may be for X-rated pictures," he shouted.

"Bernard," I replied, gesturing above his partially balding head, "there are posters behind you." I pointed above him to two posters. One was of Bernard, much younger, naked from the waist up, and standing with a beautiful redhead wearing jean short-shorts and a halter top. The second was of a blonde wearing a hard hat and a blue-checkered shirt, aiming a jackhammer into another girl's lower parts.

Bernard laughed and said, without looking at the posters, "I know. I just wanted to make that clear. This isn't only for modeling but for videos. Whatever you feel comfortable doing."

He smiled soothingly. He wasn't the sweating pervert I'd expected. Not at all like the men who came to me when I whored briefly in New York.

"Have you done any modeling before?" he asked.

"No. I thought you didn't need experience."

He held up his hand in defense. "You don't. I was just asking. You're pretty enough to have been a model."

I thanked him.

"Let's go into the other room," he said.

We walked down a short hallway covered in the same yellow paint as the office, which shined like light. He brought me into another room. This room was light blue. An off-white sheet hung over the back wall. The room was bare except for a brown leather armchair and two umbrella lights standing next to a camera on a tripod—just as I had imagined it, just like when you saw a TV movie about a fashion model. Bernard flicked a switch and the umbrellas sprang to life, giving off a fiery heat and a white light as bright as two stars.

Bernard seemed pleased that I was struck by the lights. He shook his head and looked at them as well.

"Let me take your measurements," he said. He went to a red toolbox sitting in the corner of the room and searched through it. "Shit. I don't know where the soft tape went. Dammit. We'll have to use this." He held up a metal tape measure. "It'll have to do."

He stared at me for a second, up and down, and I wondered if I should have been posing. "You're very pretty," he said absently. "Take off your clothes."

My body tensed up. It's not like I was opposed to stripping in front of him. I knew when I answered the ad that I was going to be asked to take off my clothes, or something more. It's just that when you hear those words, "Take off your clothes," part of you wants to resist no matter who you are.

Bernard saw that I was uncomfortable. "I've seen four thousand naked women in my time," he said. "I'm like a doctor. Don't worry about it. I'm here to help you."

I took off my T-shirt with an advertisement for Frank and Tommy's Pizza and my short blue skirt—I wasn't wearing too much anyway.

"Can you take your bra off?" he said.

"Sure," I said and unstrapped it with one hand. I wasn't proud of many things but I was proud of my body. It had got me into a fuck of trouble but it also had people looking at me like Bernard was looking at me now.

"You're beautiful," he said.

He took my measurements with the tape measure. The metal tape bent awkwardly as he tried to round the curves. But he got the job done and measured me at 35-24-35.

"I need to take some pictures of you for the files," he said.

I walked to the white sheet and umbrellas.

Bernard struggled with the tripod, trying to separate the legs and make it level. And then he began taking pictures. I stood in front of the camera for a moment, frozen. I felt awkward, more naked than I already was. Then I relaxed and slowly started posing. I imagined an audience, silently awed.

I had been abused and misused throughout my life. But I never forgot that sex was a beautiful thing. So I didn't feel guilty or immoral posing for Bernard. I was a sexual creature as much as I was human. I had been, my entire life. Plain and simple, I liked fucking. And I was taken in by the camera's eye. So many other girls had come into Bernard's office to do the very same thing, smiling and eager and proud and doing something Daddy would frown on but every other man would lust after. It wasn't any cold, callous waitressing job. Small beads of sweat were beginning to form on my body, a hot, arousing, sexual sweat.

Bernard took pictures of my tits and my face when I gave my best pouting looks. When he thought I was comfortable enough he told me to sit on the armchair and spread my legs. I opened my legs and smiled. Bernard mumbled, "Good. Real good. You're a natural." He looked up from the camera. "Jesus, that line must sound stupid and standard but, by God, I really do think you're a natural." He took a few more pictures of me spreading my clit hood with my fingers and said, "That will be enough."

He thanked me and I thanked him. My heart pounded. I was feeling a little high from all the heat and activity. We left the room, went back down the yellow hallway, and sat back down at his wide, wooden desk.

"I want you to know what you're getting into," he said, picking at a pencil with his fingernails. "I don't want to ruin people. This business is very hard and if you're not prepared for it, it can fuck you. I don't want my girls to get fucked, as it were. That's why I never hire junkies. If they become junkies after I hire them, there's nothing I can do about it, but I don't look for girls who are easy to control. I like a girl who seems to know what she's doing. I'm in the business of beauty. I sell health products. Only healthy girls can sell health products. There are other people in the business who will hire anybody and don't give a shit if they lose their mind or drown. Now, I'm not telling you this to get anyone in trouble. I just want you to know that you're in good hands with me. I've been around. I know the scene. I've been in two thousand fuck films myself. I'm one of the smart people in this business, which, to be honest, can sometimes think at a third-grade level. I will be good to you. You're probably lucky that you called me instead of someone else. No, I'd say you are definitely lucky."

"Well—"

"I don't think you're going to have much of a problem. You seem like a strong girl. We're outlaws," Bernard continued. "From a brutal, brutal society." He looked somberly down at his desk. "I think I have a job for you now."

"Today?"

"Yeah. Is that all right? Can you start today?"

"Sure, I just didn't think I would be starting today."

"Well, this isn't a normal job."

"No."

"There's a movie being filmed at Dick's house in San Fernando that needs another girl. Are you ready for it?"

"Yes."

"Five hundred dollars."

"What?"

"Five hundred dollars. That's what it pays."

"Sure as hell, I'm ready for it."

Bernard told me that I was supposed to meet his partner, Jay, at Dick's house. "If I'm the brains of the operation," he said, "then Jay is the muscle." Dick's full name was Dick Richards. He was one of the few male stars.

I almost got lost following Bernard's handwritten directions. I was flustered, thinking, *where the fuck am I taking myself?*

Once off the freeway I found myself in a residential neighborhood. It was quiet and green with two-story houses, something out of a postcard. Dick's house was across the street from a grocery store and a gas station. There was another freeway off in the distance. I parked and stared at the house. It was two stories tall with an upstairs deck that looked over a side yard. The house was blue. In the front yard there was an actual white picket fence. It was nicer than my parents' house.

I stood on the front porch for a full minute, my finger paused on the doorbell and wondering if I should return to my car. But then I thought about what I would be returning to and the $500, so I rang the bell.

A man opened the door wearing a tank top with tight, faded jeans and no shoes. His feet were bronze with blond hair curled on the toes. "You Shirley?" he asked.

"Yes."

"Bernie called. We've been expecting you."

He was stone-faced and moved out of the doorway to let me pass. I walked into the house, through a carpeted living room with a large stone fireplace to a small backyard with lawn chairs. A plastic rubber duck sat on a table. The house was quiet.

"Everybody's upstairs," he said. "I'm Dick, by the way." He didn't put out a hand to shake. He didn't quite meet my eye.

"It's good to meet you," I said.

"Yeah," he replied. "Why don't we go upstairs."

I followed him up tan-carpeted stairs to a bedroom. The only thing in the room was a bed with no blankets. A man with a mustache was putting a tape into a video camera on a tripod.

Another guy, deeply tan and wearing only shorts, was sitting in a director's chair with his hands in his lap. He was staring solemnly at the camera. He looked up at me and didn't change his expression.

"This is Johnny and Jay," Dick said. "Jay, this is Shirley."

The man at the camera set the videotape on the bed and looked at me. "Hey, Shirley," he said in a friendly way. "Bernie told me you were something special." He smiled at me. He had one tooth missing toward the back on the top. I could see what Bernard meant when he called Jay the muscle of the business. Jay was tall and had long, hairy arms, and one of the biggest heads I'd ever seen.

"That's Johnny Boyle," Jay said, pointing to the guy in the director's chair. "You'll be working with him later."

"Hello, Johnny," I said, hoping to sound friendly.

Johnny stared back at me, expressionless.

"Katy and Rebecca are in the bathroom," Jay said. "You should go in there and meet them. I won't have you doing very much today. Maybe just one scene. We wanted you to see how

it all works. Bernie raved about you." He smiled big again and
showed his missing tooth, a drug dealer's smile. "He was right to.
You sure are a pretty one."

"Thank you," I said and looked at Dick and Johnny, who were
frowning.

"I've got some set-up work to do," Jay said. "Why don't you
go find Katy and Rebecca. Just go knock on the door."

"It's the door left of the master bedroom," Dick said, darkly.

I walked down a short hall trying not to think about the two
frowning men and knocked on the bathroom door.

A young girl wearing a white robe opened the door. "Hi," she
said cheerily and let me in.

Sitting on the closed toilet was a woman who I immediately
thought was ugly. She had a fat nose and thin lips and brittle, frizzy
hair. She also had a gap between her two front teeth. Nothing
looks so trashy as a gap in the teeth.

"Who are you?" she said, not unfriendly.

"I'm Shirley. Who are you?"

"I'm Rebecca," said Trashy. "But call me Becca. And that's
Katy."

Katy blinked at me bright-eyed. "Have you ever done a movie
before?" she said.

"No. This is my first time."

"What fun, a rookie," said Becca.

"There's a few things that have to be done," Katy said. "Are
you shaved?"

"Shaved?"

"Is your pussy shaved? Down there." She pointed.

"No. I hadn't thought of it."

"That's all right. I'll do it for you. Lay down on the floor."

I stared briefly at her fresh-faced smile. Then I pulled down my skirt and lay on the floor. And just like that I was on the floor with another woman kneeling over me with a razor. "Do you want it all off, or just regular?" Katy asked.

I thought about it. "Um—make it as thin a line as you can make it," I said.

"OK," she giggled. "It will be like art."

She got a bottle of something off the counter and spread it around. Then she started shaving me. She stuck her tongue out and bit it rigidly in a great gesture of concentration.

"You've got a beautiful body," she said.

Katy gently brought the razor over my skin and rinsed me off. I leaned forward to look down at myself. "Stay back," she said. "Just one more thing. Close your eyes." I lay back and closed my eyes.

Katy ran her tongue from my neck to my stomach, then from my hand slowly up my arm to the other hand. And then she went down on me. I sat up to stop her but then I let it happen. It felt good but strange. I tried not to think about how I'd just met Katy and that Becca was watching. I trembled on the bathroom tile.

Katy stopped as abruptly as she had started and said, "You're done. Save it for later. I think you'll do fine."

I opened my eyes. I sat up and looked down. I had a clean straight line of pubic hair no more than a centimeter wide.

"Thank you," I said. "That was nice. I was getting worried. It seems some of the men here aren't very friendly."

"Don't mind them," Becca said. "A lot of the men have their own dicks up their ass. Stunt cocks with the ego of Picasso. In a way it's us against them. You'll learn about all of this. You'll learn a hell of a lot. I've said that you'll live more before your twenty-fifth birthday than most people live in a lifetime."

"Just like the army!" Katy said, grinning.

We all went into the bedroom to start filming. Becca and Katy walked to the bed. They were going to have a scene with Dick Richards. Katy took off her white robe. She was wearing pink lingerie over a red bra and G-string. Trashy was wearing acid-washed tight jeans and a plain white T-shirt. Jay said, "Rolling," and the scene began.

"We've been looking for the perfect cock," Katy said, sitting on the bed. "We've been going city to city testing out different guys. Let's see how you measure up." And then they started. Katy and Trashy both went down on Dick. Then he went down on Katy while Katy went down on Trashy. Then he fucked Katy while Katy and Trashy kissed with sharp cardboard tongues, as if they didn't really want to be kissing at all. I watched from behind the camera guy. It all shocked me at first. I'd never in my life watched another person having sex. But after a while it became like watching sports. It was unlike any sex I'd ever had. They were so fast, fake, and machine-like. It was like watching one of those old films from the early part of the century where people moved so fast they didn't seem real.

I think the purpose of the day was to see if I'd get scared and run away. I didn't. After an hour of watching the same scene over and over again as they taped slightly different versions, I thought the sex seemed as common as eating. When it was time for my scene, I was ready. This was what I was here for. I stripped naked and walked up to the bed. Katy rubbed my back and said, "You'll do fine," and gave me an encouraging smile.

I had one blow job scene with the guy named Johnny Boyle. I wasn't attracted to him because he was as cold as Dick Richards, but he went down on me for five minutes. After he came on my tits I said, "You're not the cock I was looking for, but in my book you're pretty good." It was my first line in a movie. In the end I enjoyed myself, even more than taking pictures with Bernard.

This was real. This was going to be seen by a lot of people.

The film was called *Moby Cock*. Bernard himself had written the script. It was about a pack of women who were searching for the perfect cock, hunting the Great White Cock. Bernard considered himself an intellectual. The search had ended with Dick Richards—an even ten inches. The story climaxes when Becca, Katy, and I agree that Dick Richards is the Great White Cock and we all do it with him at once. At the end of the day Jay said I did well and he'd give a good report to Bernard.

I didn't know how lucky I was at the time to have my first film be a Dick Richards movie. There weren't that many bona fide male stars. That film was one of the reasons my star rose so quickly.

That night, I walked out of the house into the searing valley heat with a money order for $525 in my pocket and the memory of everybody saying I was beautiful. I saw a Sizzler across from the house with all its dull fluorescent light and there was no doubt in my mind where I would be coming in to work tomorrow.

Bernard gave me another job on a Jenny Highsmith movie called *Sexi Drivers*. I played a taxi driver who worked for Jenny. She was the dispatcher. The cab drivers went around looking for sex instead of fares. I had a scene with Jenny and a full scene with a guy named Lucas Palmer. He was younger than most of the male actors. He was twenty-two and looked seventeen. He was thin and hairless. A full scene meant that I go down on him, he goes down on me, we go down on each other 69, he rides me, I ride him, and then there was the money shot—the equivalent of getting the bad guy at the end of a cop movie, or a family reunited in a sentimental movie.

Filming was standard. No more than three cameras, no more than two umbrella lights. Most of the time there was only one camera and no umbrella lights, but this was a Jenny Highsmith movie. It was still shot on ugly video, but done with more care.

We filmed at Jenny's place. Jenny was rich enough to have her own mansion in the hills and another small house in West Hollywood. The house in West Hollywood was her personal studio where she filmed her movies. It was in a suburban neighborhood with a Spanish tile roof and a green front lawn. Young parents walked their kids in strollers on the clean sidewalk while we fucked inside.

Jenny had a fan club of close to a million. That meant that anytime one of her movies came out, a million people bought it and she got a percentage. A video went for at least $19.95, probably more. Do the math and you'll understand why there are so many people in pornography. Jenny had won the best actress award four times. She could make $5,000 a night stripping as a superstar. The marquee at the Hot Box read, THE QUEEN HAS ARRIVED. JENNY HIGHSMITH, TWO NIGHTS ONLY. She was royalty.

When I met Jenny Highsmith I lost any doubts I may have had about working in porn. She was pretty and self-assured and healthy, the most naturally attractive person I had ever seen, red-haired, blue-eyed, smooth-skinned, without implants. She fucked hard for a living but that didn't bother her for a moment. She was happier than most people, and guiltless. She was a businesswoman with pride and drive. After working with her I lost my last shadow of self-judgment and fell deeply into the work.

Sexi Drivers took three days to shoot and two weeks to edit and package. Bernard said that the whole movie probably cost $10,000 and would make a hundred times that. He usually didn't talk business with the girls but he said he liked me. He said I had something more than promise.

I would soon become accustomed to all the business and politics of the porn industry. Pay rates weren't as high at first. If I could have gotten royalties on my first two films, I could have retired at twenty-three. But all actors start out at a flat fee. You start as hamburger and work your way up to filet mignon. Sometimes they stuff a whole wad of cash in a girl's hand after her first time, to keep her interested. Then the pay goes down. They tell her later that that was just a very good day, we were feeling generous. The pay scale normally goes from $400 for guy-girl, $500 for girl-girl, $700 for anal, $1,000 for double penetration or a private video, to $1,500 for a gang bang. I was brand new so I made under scale, but more than anything I'd ever made at any other job in my life. This was no seedy, cheap affair. This was clean and comfortable. I had finally left the dry land of bad jobs.

I never became a junky. Nothing violent inspired me to get involved in porn. I just had the gun of boredom and poverty to my head.

Almost overnight, I was a new animal. You do only one fuck film and you're never the same person. Now that I was starting something of a new career, I was filled with a rush of new emotion. I wasn't one of those girls who got into the industry because they looked for abuse, or they just weren't very smart. I wasn't one of those girls whose only asset was her body and fell into porn in a sad, inevitable way. I had fine self-esteem. I knew exactly what I wanted to do with my life. And I knew that I wanted to be treated decently. I'd received more abuse from customers at a restaurant than from the people inside Bernard's house in the hills. I had learned nothing from waiting tables except how to balance four plates on one arm.

There was some sacrifice. To have so much sex with so little love, a person has to shut off her emotions. Sex is difficult to perform if you don't mean it. We were like machines. Now, that's not saying machines couldn't have a good time. But I mean, if I was giving my fifth blow job of the day and it was eleven o'clock at night, I went at it with a businesslike dedication. I was exhausted but I was getting paid. It was my job. Just another cock coming down the factory line.

Hooker Booker

K. St. Germaine

"Hello."

"Is Tiffany there?"

"This is Tiffany," I say in my sultriest voice. "Who's this?"

"Um, this is John."

They're all named John. They know what they are.

"Hi, John," I purr. "What's up?"

I wasn't making ends meet as a circus sideshow starlet/fire-eater, and it was starting to look like I'd end up waitressing, again. Since there is *nothing* more degrading than waitressing, I teamed up with a girlfriend from my porn store clerk days and we decided to look into escorting. It seemed like a great idea at the time. We were two cute girls with very few hang-ups, and when we did things together we felt invincible.

We each went on a couple of "dates," only to find that we

were just no good at prostitution. It wasn't for lack of trying; I just didn't like meeting up with middle-aged businessmen in sleazy airport hotel bars, and she was a lesbian who had no idea how to give a blow job.

But even though we were miserable failures as prostitutes, we managed to land jobs as hooker bookers—women who arranged "dates" between sex workers and clients. I knew I'd be a good booker because I had two important requirements: an incredibly sexy phone voice, and knowledge of many areas of the adult industry. Besides having been a porn store clerk, I'd been a telephone sex "therapist" for over a year for Los Angeles public access television personality Dr. Susan Block, and was bartender at her swingers' club-speakeasy. I was also a fire-eating, glass-dancing stripper for upscale orgies at mansions in the Hollywood Hills, and had dipped my own toes into "sex for money" quite successfully in the form of a lovely sugar daddy in Malibu. I felt qualified in spades.

I went to my interview in an office building on the outskirts of Glendale, a bland suburb ten miles from Hollywood. Alex, a tall twenty-six-year-old, first-generation upper-class Bombay Indian immigrant-cum-wannabe gangster, interviewed me. He asked me about my experience booking. I told him I had none in booking, exactly, but that hustling these guys would be like "shooting fish in a barrel." So within twenty-four hours of saying, "I want to…" I found myself dutifully, gainfully employed.

The setup was simple: a desk, a phone, and a television, all in one room for the booker, and an outer office where the dispatchers (i.e., the baby pimps) ran the girls and their drivers. The johns would respond to ads for escorts that ran in various independent city papers and several adult websites. All the girls featured in the ads—Amber, Alicia, Mona, Vanessa, and so on—had different "personalities," looks, styles, and telephone numbers. All of which rang through to the single phone on my desk.

The ad-girls' names were coded to indicate what they looked like. For example, if "my" name began with an *A*—Ashley, Alicia, Amber—I had to portray a blonde with overlarge breasts. A *T* name would be a busty brunette, a *C* name meant an Asian girl, and so on. The johns would call looking for the best deal, so intentionally I made it seem like either the first girl or the last they called was the best hooker value. Since I had caller ID, I could tell when each guy was calling back, and I changed my voice for each call to impersonate the appropriate nonexistent escort he was calling for. Of course the girls in the pictures were never real—they were stock photos bought off the Internet to be used exactly for this reason.

The girls who worked for my company came from every race and background. They were the cream of the midlevel crop—which is actually not saying much, but they each had their features. LaToya was a thirty-eight-year-old thick black woman with enormous knockers. Rosario, a skinny Hispanic girl, didn't speak English but was very sweet. Christina was a blonde Goth chick with bad teeth and a great ass. Valerie, a brunette in the Wilshire district, sported fake DDs. Our prize jewel, Fiona Peaches, was a genuine porn star. None of these women looked anything like the photos advertised—but if they were good at the hustle, they could make the trick work.

It was not unheard of to walk into the office and find some naked girl under hot lights with her legs spread wide open for a camera. There were always new girls coming in to interview for escort jobs—they showed up in the tiniest outfits, reeking of cheap perfume. We had them fill out an application, then get naked in the outer office for their requisite photo session. We posted some pictures of each woman on our website, and sold the rest as stock photos. The entire office would smell of Eau de Would-Be-Prostitute for hours afterward.

It was my job to make sure these all girls were kept busy with johns. That was it. I chatted up the callers responding to our ads, found out who they were, what they did, where they worked, what part of town they were at, and what they were interested in sexually—at least, for that evening or afternoon. This was necessary to avoid psychos, or cops. On a typical night I'd field at least a hundred calls (nearly all were men, though once in a while a randy lesbian would call us up for a date). Technically, it was my job to lie—and lie as professionally as possible. The johns were looking for an independent escort, not a hooker booker at a cattle-call agency. If I hesitated for a second in my responses to their questions (typically asinine, trying to get a bargain), they sensed immediately that I was with an agency and hung up.

I said anything I thought these men wanted to hear to make a sale. I had big tits. I was really horny and had a shaved pussy. I was bored and alone in my house and playing with myself. All the callers were looking to get laid and they wanted to hear me make that offer. There are catchwords in this business that I'd need to carefully avoid during my phone conversations with the johns, such as "full service" and "girlfriend experience," which are illegal to say, and if careless I could end up in the middle of a vice sting. To get around this, I simply said I was a "full escort." Two words that are still legal and yet told them nothing. But they *thought* they heard "full service."

They'd always want it for around $150. Our rates were anywhere from $120 to $500 depending on the girl and the night. The average rate was $200, just to get them in the door. Now, this rate was for an exotic one-on-one, in-call striptease—and maybe a hand job or nude massage—but I promised them nothing on the phone, while of course subtly promising "everything" to get them in, and get their clothes off. The moment the john arrived, the girls would work him for another few hundred if they wanted to get laid or a blow job. I made ten percent of the final transaction, plus tips from the girls.

Always on staff were Alex, the head pimp, and his co-pimps, Jason, Mike, and Chauncey—geeky wannabe gangster types who were into "Dungeons and Dragons" and computer gaming. They had found their way into the pimping business through websites, and were looking to score their "American dream" SUVs through the skin trade, as well as dealing in low-grade pot and forged sports autographs on eBay. Because of their inexperience, they consistently got the run-around by a dozen or so hookers. They tried to keep the business as legal as possible with their "don't ask, don't tell" policy with the women. For my own devious entertainment, and extra cash, I took it on myself to see how far the girls would go. For example, if I had a guy on the phone who wanted a golden shower, I would (completely illegally) book this activity and send him to my girl Christina, who would piss on his face for $400. I would make a solid $40 for the booking, and Christina would tip me out another $40 to $80 for ten minutes of work that was actually very little work for her.

I got calls from seemingly everyone in Los Angeles. With the caller ID, I usually knew whom I was talking to before I even picked up the phone. The lunchtime rush from the movie studios was always a profitable event. As soon as I would see movie studio names on my caller ID, the price would go up another $200—and the trick would always go through. I had everyone from producers to grips running to valley hotels for their noontime trysts. I also had tons of musicians from famous bands calling—and they were some of the best *and* the worst tricks. I couldn't even get girls to go to some of them after a while because the rockers and rappers were so nasty and coked out. I booked tons of lawyers, who were the stingiest tricks, and of course a lot of writers (the poor shut-ins!), and an overwhelming number of construction workers. But, as cliché as it sounds, the bulk of our business was from out-of-town businessmen in hotels. These were my favorite clients—because they were so eager to get away from their wives and families, I could charge them ridiculously high fees.

Generally the tricks (or *whackers,* as we liked to call them) were well behaved. Especially if they were veteran johns. Those were my preferred clients. They knew that they never get the girl in the picture; it was a nice, honest transaction. It was the newcomers I always had to watch out for. These fools would go to the back of the *LA Weekly* and really think that they were going to hook up with a gorgeous blonde model for $150 and get a full-service escort. My girls would never fuck anything for $150—think triple that figure, and you're back in reality.

Sometimes when the novice whacker got to the room and found out he'd get nothing more than a striptease and *maybe* a hand job for $150, he'd become so angry he'd be on the verge of violence. I would have to call him back and calm him down by apologizing for my terribly uptight hooker, and promise him full service at another random location—then get him and the girl out of that hotel as quickly as possible. I'd have her set up with another guy in a different San Fernando Valley location in twenty minutes, and the angry john would be fifteen miles away in Burbank searching for a fictional hotel at a nonexistent address.

Most of the calls came in for "Ashley," a busty, blonde model in one of our ads. More often than not, only "LaToya" would be working. LaToya was tucked neatly away in an apartment building in Sherman Oaks. I would book the call regardless, and send the client on a wild goose chase through the valley, purposely getting him lost, all while telling him sweet nothings on his cell phone to keep him good and warmed up. By the time he got to LaToya's house he'd be so worked up that the trick would go through, regardless. This tactic had a success rate of about 90 percent.

After eight months I was ready for a change of scenery—and higher commissions. I started searching out new escort agencies. I found one guy, way out in Calabasas, who advertised as letting the bookers work from home. This man was so sleazy (in a midlife crisis sort of way), that he actually tried to turn me out to escort for him. No deal. The next place I tried was full of Hollywood street punks who took their ratty children to work with them. Finally, I found a place in North Hollywood that seemed so hilariously underbelly I couldn't resist. It was owned by a young Armenian gangster named Arthur, whose office was appropriately filled with *Godfather* and *Scarface* posters. The woman who ran the office, Genny, was a pro madame from England, who affected a convincing Valley Girl accent while working the phones. They hired me immediately, and within twelve hours of looking for a new job I was on the clock at my new place of employment.

Here we had an office full of hookers, drivers, and gangsters—a cornucopia of nefariousness. Our escorts were great—they either put out, or carried off extraordinary rip-off schemes.

My favorite girl was Anita; I would send her out for the johns who pissed me off. Anita could rip off anyone. A beautiful girl with cocoa skin and big green eyes, she would make the whacker feel at ease, get the money, and tell him she was running the cash out to her driver outside. She would leave a cell phone and a sweater to make it look like she was coming back, and then as soon as she got to the car, screech off into the night. The confused john would call back, looking for her, never even considering that the cell phone and sweater had been ripped off from a previous trick and that he'd been had. I'd calm him down and give him our code name for the "manager," tell him to call tomorrow for a refund, and explain that I would fire that girl immediately. Sometimes they would call for a solid week before they figured it out.

It was not unheard of for any one of our distinguished ladies to pass the time by giving her driver a top-notch blow job while waiting on tricks at the hotel. They would also use blow jobs to jockey for favored position within the agency. In fact, within this business, blow jobs were standard office currency. All the girls would suck off Arthur the Pimp, and then fight among themselves about it later. I would hear about all of this on rides home in Arthur's Mercedes SUV. He would chuckle about it and then call them all dirty whores under his Marlboro-soaked breath.

Every night during my shift, a gaggle of gangsters would arrive in slick-looking suits to play cards with Arthur, gambling away thousands of dollars while smoking hundreds of cigarettes. I would be shut in this tiny two-room office with the boys, barely able to breathe between the stench of Marlboros and heavily perfumed whores. And every night it was a constant battle to get those fuckers out of there so I could run their business. At the same time, our main driver, Russell, would be "interviewing" prospective new escorts in the inner office while I was hustling the johns on the phone and filling out the call sheets.

I was running fifteen tricks a shift, sometimes working eighteen-hour stints—and I finally burned out. I'd had enough of the pimps, the whores, the scoundrels, and the whackers. I was completely turned off by the whole idea of getting anyone laid—even myself. I was taking in the problems of every man in Los Angeles who couldn't get laid by his wife or anyone else for free. Lying had become second nature, and then passé. I really started to freak out when I realized I hadn't had sex for months.

I walked out the door from my last shift and knew that I couldn't go back, simply for my own sexual well-being. I'd been at it too long—for nearly a year—and it was starting to show in my commissions. I just didn't care anymore. Besides, I had started to run men in my personal life the same way I ran johns. I worked them over for freebies, and looked shrewdly at each and every one of them as a mark, scheduling them in for free lunches and dinners. I had three dates a day scheduled around prime shopping and entertainment hours. In turn, I could only truly appreciate men who were running some kind of a game, too. I had lost faith in the male sex, and I was feeling a bit misanthropic about romance, to say the least.

I recently saw one of the escorts out at the El Coyote restaurant in Hollywood, chain smoking cigarettes with a rich couple, dressed better than ever, looking great. I remembered how she said she loved her work, and was always willing to "take one for the team." We met eyes at the same time, and then quickly looked away. She was on a job and I was on a date, so naturally neither one of us wanted to publicly greet the other. But she looked as if she'd moved up the hooker scale, and I was happy for her. I gave her a wink as I left.

South Bronx, Sex Ed
Ellen Friedrichs

Paulo is getting beat up at home because his mom thinks he's gay. Tonya Green's belly grows daily, due to a few encounters with the thirty-year-old homeless guy who sleeps on her stoop and sometimes in her bed. Maria is sporting a gash down the side of her face, the result of an encounter with a broken bottle wielded by another girl bitter over Maria's alleged behavior with her man. Brandi is trying to find a place to live because she can't stay at home anymore with a grandfather who keeps touching her. And me? Me, I'm standing in front of these kids, plastic package in one hand, banana in the other, looking for volunteers to demonstrate the proper way to put on a condom.

I teach sex ed in the South Bronx at an after-school program. None of my kids get sex ed at school. A few have had health classes. But even fewer have learned anything in them. This isn't surprising, as sex ed in public schools in this country is becoming a thing of the past. That's not to say that the government won't give you a significant amount of cash to teach what it claims is sex ed. But most sex educators I know don't buy that telling kids to pledge virginity and abstinence to a very Christian-sounding God is actually sex ed. Neither is denying that kids are queer and need condoms and have orgasms and masturbate and will do these things whether they learn about them in school or not.

None of my kids come to the program for the sex ed, of course. Some come because it is free and they get dinner. Some come because their parents are hoping it will help them stay away from the gangs that they walk ten blocks out of their way to avoid, and some are court ordered to be there. My kids are all black and Latino. I'm white and Jewish and, even more alien to them, Canadian. To stay in the program they have to attend the sex ed class once a week and meet with me one on one. During meetings they sit sullenly, they doodle, or they talk. When they do they say things like: "Last week I had sex in a closet at my cousin's birthday party." "My brother's in Rikers, I think they're fucking him up pretty bad in there." "How do you give a guy a hand job?" "That movie you showed about the kid with AIDS? I'm sorry, Miss. That was mad homo."

Mad homo. It applies to a lot of things. The fact that I told them they couldn't call each other *fag* or *gay* as an insult, for example, is mad homo. So is the fact that I kick them out if the guys call the girls *bitches* or if the girls punch each other in the arms and say, "Shut the fuck up!" when they disagree. "Miss," they explain when I intervene. "Miss, that's just how we talk together. We're just playin'. You don't understand." I tell them fine, you're right, I don't. But I still make them do an exercise in which they have to compliment the person sitting to their left and wait patiently as they mumble through: *Maria, I like your shirt; Anton, you're a good basketball player; Philip, you're a nice friend.*

Forcing compliments out of these kids has its merit, but it doesn't immediately change the social and sexual interaction of the group. I come into class one day as the kids are hearing about the blow job Manny recently received. Manny is a huge, towering kid who's sixteen but looks twenty-five. He's explaining how he needs head but would never reciprocate on a girl. "Dick ain't nasty like pussy," he concludes. All the guys agree noisily, with commentary. I debate jumping in. It's not the language. The kids know my rule: Use slang as long as you can show me you know the real word. You want to say *dick?* First prove you know *penis, scrotum,* and *testicle.* You want to say *pussy?* Only if you explain the different parts of the vulva without forgetting the clitoris. I don't feel like making Manny run through the drill again, but I decide the conversation warrants at least a perfunctory interjection. So I tell them, "Nobody's genitals are nasty and there definitely isn't anything gross about the vulva. Oral sex is just a matter of personal preference."

Chaos ensues. The boys practically jump on top of each other trying to tell me just how wrong I am, just how homo it is to go down on a girl, just under how much duress they would need to be to ever consider doing that. But they want me to understand that, if a girl ever refused them head, that's it, they're through. I know some of it is posturing. But I also know a lot isn't. As Jefferson puts it, "If a girl I'm with don't give me head, I say *see ya,* take her cellie, and erase my number." I'm busy organizing the lesson but I look up again to say, "This might work for you now, but no grown woman is going to put up with that. Good luck in the future." I hear one of the girls, maybe Carmen, say, "Awww, shit! Jefferson, you got burned!" I don't actually know if my statement is true or not and if these girls will grow up to demand oral sex, but I figure it can't hurt to make them think that.

Then I hand out worksheets and announce that today's session is on values and morals. The kids prefer classes that involve condom demos, or pictures of sexually transmitted infections and games where they have to scramble to answer questions like: *How many hours after unprotected sex can a woman take emergency contraception?* However, sometimes I like to make them actually talk to each other. So, now they must debate the merits and drawbacks of sex without commitment and whether a girl is a slut if she carries condoms and should gay teens be allowed to take same-sex partners to school dances. "Miss, we don't even get art class, you think we're going to get a *dance?*" says Tina. It's a good point, so I tell her, "In theory, then, just in theory."

Of course most things for these kids aren't theoretical. Like Amelia Gonzales's pregnancy. That is pretty real. "Amelia," I say when she tells me, "you came to all my classes. What happened?" And fourteen-year-old Amelia, who is heavy and wears baggy overalls and whom I have heard the boys refer to as Austin Powers's "Fat Bastard," just mumbles through her braces, "I dunno." But eventually it comes out: Amelia is in foster care. She lives with a woman she calls her grandmother and two of her seven siblings. Her mom has drug problems and is not allowed to see her. The grandmother hates her. She calls her ugly. And she hasn't done Amelia's hair since she was seven. The boy is older, sixteen. He's from down the block. "So," I say, trying hard not to come off as the condescending teacher I am pretty sure I sound like, "you kind of wanted this baby? You think a baby will love you and be cute and cuddle with you when you're sad?" Amelia looks at me and says, "No, I don't. My doctor just says I can't have an abortion."

Then she tells me how her doctor has explained abortion. According to him the procedure is physically excruciating and often results in fully grown babies descending into the toilet piece by bloody piece after the inevitable botched operation. And even if this does not occur, the screams of infants being ripped limb from limb will echo in the head of the forever damaged mother. I tell Amelia this is not the way abortions work and ask her why she thinks her doctor would give her such misinformation. Amelia explains that the doctor is mad at her for getting pregnant. He thinks she should have the baby and has told her if she has an abortion she will feel such guilt that she will no doubt end up on drugs like her mother. I tell Amelia that if she wants to have an abortion she can do so and explain that she won't be expelling bloody chunks of baby. That abortion is confidential for teens in New York. That she can go to a different provider. That she doesn't have to tell her doctor, her grandmother, her social worker, or the boy. That she can get it covered by emergency Medicaid and that I will go with her if she decides to do it and is nervous. But I am not surprised the next week when she chooses to continue the pregnancy, explaining that the sixteen-year-old father promises to support her.

At the end of the year we get a grant. I can train ten kids to become HIV peer educators and can pay them to do so. I pick Manny and Brandi and Tina and Jefferson. I also pick Amelia, whose grandmother tells me on the phone, "You really want Amelia? She's no good at anything." I pick LaToya James, who is amazingly quiet and wears her Catholic school uniform to program every day despite the fact that all the other kids mock her mercilessly. I pick Rina Lee, who bursts with energy and thinks sex is gross but who regularly asks what it feels like to kiss a boy. I pick Paulo, who came to school last week with a broken tooth after being jumped once again. I pick Jenny Estrada, who is scared to take the subway alone to her dentist appointments in Manhattan. And I pick José Mendez, who wants so badly to be hard and tells me about all the gang members he's friends with, but who talks really quietly when he explains that he can't remember his sister's name because she lives with his dad whom he hasn't seen in five years. I take this group of kids from my sex ed classes and tell them, "You guys are going to be the teachers. You are going to go around to other schools and teach kids the way I teach you. Think you can handle it?" And Manny and Brandi and Tina and Jenny and Jefferson and LaToya and Amelia and José and Paulo and Rina all look skeptical. But after some coaxing they decide that they can indeed get up in front of a group and talk seriously about a subject that they normally only encounter as a punch line. They decide that they can explain that not only gay people get AIDS, that casual contact won't pass the virus, that getting tested is important, that condoms work. They decide this and then they deliver. And watching them in action kind of makes up for the fact that Marcy is pregnant again, and Raymond got busted for selling drugs, and Monica's mom won't let her come back to the program because a boy called her house. And it kind of makes up for the fact that even if teaching sex ed in this country is an uphill battle, sometimes it's a hill worth climbing.

Visiting Kinsey
Carol Queen

I'm not sure when I first heard of Alfred C. Kinsey, but I do know that I cleared out an entire round dinner table of dorm-mates my freshman year in college by reading out loud from *Sexual Behavior in the Human Male*. It was too darn hot to eat weird dormitory casserole as I recited the percentages of urban versus rural youth who had sported with animals. "Farm animals, mostly," I added helpfully as I studied the statistical tables in the book's appendix. "It's the reason more farm kids have done it." But when I looked up, all my fellow diners were gone, vanished—*voop!*—like sheep in the field when faced with an Oregon farm boy.

Much, much later I had occasion to read the book again, and also *Sexual Behavior in the Human Female*. This time I took copious notes, because I read it for credit my first year at the Institute for Advanced Study of Human Sexuality. (I also timed myself masturbating to see whether my own personal best matched the mean time to masturbated orgasm among women; who says science isn't fun?) Kinsey's books were required reading for everyone at the school that doubtless took Kinsey more seriously than he was taken, even, at Indiana University, where the eponymous Kinsey Institute still hangs on nearly fifty years after its founder's death, in spite of the fact that, as I write, the Indiana legislature continues to try to shell the venerable institute out like a bad pea. Whatever Kinsey did to bother people when he was alive bothers them still. To me, that's a basic reason to idolize him and to want to visit the institute.

Let's back up just in case you don't keep up with 20th-century sexological gods (and contemporary cinema).

What Kinsey did, basically, was count. First he counted gall wasps, and collected so many that he established himself, in true early-20th-century fashion, as a Really Big Sex Geek. Then in 1938 he was tapped to teach a class about marriage at Indiana U. Sexological oral history suggests that IU was glad to hire him for such an arduous task; how could a guy who'd amassed a collection of several zillion gall wasps be anything but a big dull nerd? He'd been one of the country's first Eagle Scouts and would clearly be harmless as he taught the bright-eyed married students at Indiana U. It's not as if he was going to rile anybody up.

But geeks (as we know by now) have super-powers: They're laser-focused on whatever interests them, and they want to know all there is to know about their chosen obsession. When Kinsey went to the library to prepare for his class, he found a dearth of material to work from. Hadn't anybody ever studied this sex thing before? Where was the science?

Sex became Kinsey's new gall wasp. It was the mysterious jewel with endless facets. If there wasn't good, scientific information to be had, he'd just go collect it. And for the next few decades that's what he did. He took sex histories and ran the stats; that's how he found out how many urban kids fooled around with their puppies compared to how many rural kids fooled around with their goats. He collected books, photos, diaries, artwork, and anything else that had to do with sex. He collected, he counted, and then he published. Just as students had lined up at IU to take the marriage class, people lined up to hear him speak and to buy his books. By the time he was done he had changed the world—though he never really finished his project; he died in 1956, long before he could release all the books and studies he'd planned to generate out of the nearly twenty thousand sex histories he took.

I had the honor of studying under one of Kinsey's former associates, Wardell Pomeroy, while at the Institute for Advanced Study of Human Sexuality. Pomeroy was then dean of students, if I remember correctly, and still teaching classes on how to take a Kinsey-style sex history. If the Kinsey biopic is a true indication of how things were at Indiana University while Prok (Kinsey's nickname, a contraction of "Professor Kinsey") ruled the sexuality studies institute that now bears his name, other associates got closer to the big man...a lot closer. But at IASHS in 1989 I was beyond thrilled to have Pomeroy himself take my sex history. If you've seen the movie you'll know what the history looked like: nothing more than a series of indecipherable scrawls on an otherwise empty page. The secret of the coding system was where on the page the researcher places the scrawls: Different parts of the paper are reserved for recording different sexual behaviors and experiences. Unlike some surveys, which ask whether you've ever done this or that (to which, of course, one optional answer is "No," whether you've truly done it or not), the Kinsey process was done face-to-face and encouraged people to be forthcoming and not hide possibly controversial experience. Instead of *whether,* Kinsey and his interviewers asked *when:* "How old were you when you began masturbating? How old were you when you had your first sexual experience with a male? With a female?"

I had been swinging from the chandelier as hard as possible ever since getting to the Sex Institute, plus I had been partway around the block before even getting there. I began my Kinsey-like sexual science as a teenager, when I used to tie a ribbon around my old-fashioned bedpost every time I had sex with a new person. Only one person ever looked at these and knew what they were: Born-in-the-bone sex researchers, really, are rather few and far between. But it wasn't until arriving at the Sex Institute that I learned more about Kinsey and truly became one of his spiritual daughters. (Hey, he even looked a bit like my dad, bow tie and all.)

I'd been having some adventures, so I was pleased to have something to answer in just about every category on the notoriously complete listing of sexual experience that is the Kinsey-style sex history. After we were done, Wardell and I retired to the hot tub (source of the derisive, or maybe just envious, moniker that outsiders gave the institute: "Hot Tub U"). One thing led to another, and soon I could have answered a question that wasn't on the sex history (but probably should have been): How old were you when you had sexual contact with a member of Kinsey's research team?

I told this story at my graduation, which was more like a roast than an actual ceremony. This is mainly due to the singular eccentricity of the institute's president, Ted McIlvenna, a man as influenced by the Kinsey revolution as any now alive. After recounting the other things the institute had given me, I told the Pomeroy sex history story, which was met by a bellow of indignation from Ted: "Wardell never told me that!"

"That," I said sweetly, "is because Wardell was a gentleman."

As, clearly, I am not. But look at it this way: Pomeroy has died, and I've waited until now to publish the story. And, as has been my punch line to this anecdote all along: It was as close as I could ever get to fucking Alfred C. Kinsey. I appreciate history and lineage, you know, and as an IASHS grad from the Pomeroy years I know I am in a direct line of descent from the sexual revolution that erupted at Indiana University and from which the United States has clearly not yet recovered.

(Besides, I'm not the first to think this way; reportedly, Allen Ginsberg could trace his sexual contacts all the way back to Walt Whitman, a fact that gave him enormous pride.)

A good many years thereafter I found myself among a group of sexologists climbing the stone steps at Indiana U, about to enter the hall that housed the Kinsey Institute. I was given a short tour: Here's the card catalog; here's the glass case with Freud's letter to the distressed mother of a homosexual; here's the door that, when swung open, reveals...the archives.

I could barely see the other end of the hall. It's huge, football-field-huge. Packed with acid-free boxes, ready to be filled with nitrogen if fire breaks out, full of towering shelves full of Kinsey's collection. I wasn't allowed to romp around in there; in fact, I was barely allowed to keep a pencil and paper. But I was entranced. I'm no Catholic (except, perhaps, in my tastes), but there I stood peering into my Vatican.

I gushed to the lady behind the counter: "You must love this job! I can't imagine anything so exciting and meaningful!"

She looked at me with a gimlet eye and gave a snort. "Are you kidding? All this sex!"

Only later, when coming out of the haze of shock her response engendered, did I realize how savvy a hiring policy the Kinsey

Institute had. If you staff your desk with battle-axes who have absolutely no interest in your wares, your theft level will be way near zero. No chance this mousy, middle-aged Bloomington native would get sticky with the Bettie Page playing cards.

Twenty or so minutes before closing time she warned us that we'd have to stop looking soon. Then, I guess, she let my enthusiasm thaw her chill. "You folks came a long way. Do you want to see the art?"

Did we ever! So she buttoned up a little early and took us up the elevator. The secretarial pool walls had at least a dozen large-format black-and-white photos of Kinsey and his closest associates: a young Wardell, Clyde Martin, and Paul Gebhard. My favorite pic of all showed Kinsey at the height of his fame, lecturing at UC Berkeley. You wouldn't think there were that many people in all of the United States in 1952; the place is absolutely jammed, everyone looking at him raptly. No one had ever stood before thousands of people and said what Alfred C. Kinsey had to say.

But they hadn't hung anything really fancy in the secretarial pool. Now we headed down a very long hall. This must be where others associated with the Kinsey Institute had their offices, because other staff and faculty at IU might be less than thrilled to have their corridor walls decorated by what we saw as Ms. Battle-Axe trotted us down the hall. I was able to get her to stop for a minute so that we could look at fetish and cross-dressing photographs from 1890 to about 1950: big happy guys in corsets, in slinky dresses, in sun hats. She informed us that the IU medical school had just collaborated with the Kinsey Institute in an exhibition of these. But then the power-walk resumed; she was taking us to the special art room, and we didn't have much time, and the hall was no place for lollygagging. For heaven's sake, didn't we want to see the Picassos?

Well, sure we did. But I had the distinctly surreal experience of zipping past erotic art that anywhere else would be stars of the show. "Is that a Chagall?" I gasped as we hurried past a jewel-toned scene of people fucking in midair; at least that's what it seemed to be…we passed it too fast for me to be sure, but the style was too familiar to miss. "Yes," Ms. Axe said. "We have three." And indeed they were there next to the first one—three erotic Chagalls in a neat little row.

Finally the secret museum, the sanctum sanctorum of the Kinsey Institute's art holdings. Here, thank goodness, Ms. Axe allowed us to stop and peruse, and what a lot to see! Picasso, sure—but who doesn't know he drew dirty pictures? Other well-known artists held their naughty paintings a bit closer to their vests, some keeping them, others allowing them only into the hands of trusted collectors. But my twin fascinations in the room didn't fall into this category. One, a chunk of an explicit mural from Pompeii (or was it Herculaneum), glowed softly in a glass case, its millennia-old colors faded a little. It sat right next to a very old condom box…like, four hundred years old. (Much prettier than the ones we have now, with a spicy picture painted on the porcelain.)

The other item that made my eyes go wide hung next to all the other paintings, but it wasn't a picture of fucking, or masturbating, or anything similar to the other art. It was a garish clown. I inspected it to see if it was one of those pictures full of hidden naked ladies, the kind of erotic "Where's Waldo?" that our great-granddads all loved, but saw nothing but essence of Clown—a little scary, but then, lots of people find all clown pictures frightening.

"What in the world is this?" I asked, though it had begun to dawn on me whose work it must be.

"Oh," said Ms. Axe, as though she were the docent of a completely pedestrian art gallery in a mall somewhere, "that's a John

Wayne Gacy." Gacy—who dressed as a clown for kids' birthday parties, then lured them away and lust-murdered them—was a not-incompetent clown painter, but he didn't exactly hold up to the masters whose work shared the walls with his. We were all a little freaked out to see it, but, sexologists all, we knew what it was doing there. The museum room wasn't primarily about art; like any other room at the archives, all the material shared one thing: sexological significance.

When a group of colleagues and I set out to create the San Francisco–based Center for Sex and Culture, a nonprofit archive and teaching center, we did so as Kinsey's spiritual children, just as convinced as he was that the sex-related material of our culture, so seemingly ubiquitous but really so ephemeral, is valuable and important to preserve. Like Kinsey and the subsequent holders of his legacy, we collect pretty much everything. (I am always especially jazzed at estate sales when I come upon a stash of Granddad's dirty jokes, mimeographed onto onionskin paper and somehow invariably folded into quarters to keep their true nature from being immediately observed when someone riffles through his desk.)

Alfred Kinsey collected people's sex-related papers—the magazines, the photo sets, the diaries—as if they were rare bugs. Every generation has some sort of pornography, but depictions change, and studying the changes helps scholars understand how cultural shifts affect everything from knowledge of STDs and birth control to gender roles and fetishes. And before Kinsey began to collect, the only such stashes of material truly were secret museums, amassed by mostly rich old guys who shared them with no one but maybe their friends from the club. B.K.—Before Kinsey—that was how everyone seemingly liked it. Homosexuality was in the closet, of course, before Kinsey's book *Sexual Behavior in the Human Male* told us that about a third of all men had had some homosexual contact. But more than that, pretty much *all* sex was in the metaphorical closet, certainly compared to the way we live today. We still can't be assured that the sex information we get from mainstream culture is accurate, but anyone with cable TV or a modem knows how much sex has been made available to the curious, at virtually all socioeconomic levels.

And we're still very curious. We don't get much better school-sponsored sex ed than children did in Kinsey's day. Just as adolescent and adult men, especially, once crowded around photo sets held by an especially lucky colleague, eager to see The Thing Itself, to work out the mechanics of sex in case they were ever lucky enough to have any, porn still offers itself to the curious, offering vicarious images of sex with distant and unavailable partners. No one has ever closed the closet door since Kinsey (though many have put their shoulders to it and tried), partly because the cultural repositories within which we hide our sexuality are full and spilling over. Some of us still try to hide. For the rest of us, sex has been at least partially integrated into our lives. I thank Kinsey for that too: If he had not existed it would have been necessary to invent him, for who among us can imagine America without the social changes his curiosity and single-mindedness helped to unleash?

One of the many, many things that makes the Kinsey story irresistible for a movie is its built-in drama, part of which comes from the improbability of its setting: Bloomington, Indiana. Perhaps the revelations Kinsey uncovered and publicly announced could only have been assimilated by America if they'd come from such an innocent source. Kinsey kept his job (and, for quite some time, his foundation funding) because he toiled in bucolic small-town academia, respecting scientific research and using it as a shield as he advanced into the public realm with amazing, thrilling news:

Most Americans had more involved and interesting sex lives than anyone knew.

Now might be a good moment to mention Kinsey's detractors. *Kinsey* the movie depicts the man and his milieu compassionately and well, but definitely gives people something to quack about: that he and his associates weren't as removed from their subject as good scientists should be! But that's not the Kinsey-haters' reason for trying to bring him down (a cottage industry that still flourishes today: The conservative, moralistic right wing, of which Kinsey's own father was a member, loves to hate Kinsey, which means that you have to be careful which books about him you read). No, the K-phobes hate his work because of what he revealed—sexual diversity, and a lot of it—and because of what it meant to the culture to have these things announced.

It meant, essentially, that the cat was out of the bag.

Before you knew it, McCarthy was going down. Beatniks seized the café districts of every major U.S. city, about as popular then as Goths are in small towns today (or were in the '80s). The modern homosexual rights movement was born out of the Kinsey stats, and so was the Summer of Love. Hey, you know the rest of the story. Bathhouses! Swingers! *Roe v. Wade!*

And the right wing doesn't like any of this—not one bit.

It'll be noteworthy, certainly, that the Kinsey movie shows Prok deciding to experiment first hand with same-sex love and open relationships. People may be shocked—shocked!—that he and his researchers dive right into sexual research at, er, street level. But the movie doesn't sugarcoat the effects on him, on his fabulous wife, and on his associates caused by their trying to live by a new set of mores. Any one of us doing the same today knows it takes some experimentation, as well as some savvy, to figure out how to deal with jealousy, guilt, and the opprobrium of others. If the

Kinsey team really was living as far outside the box as their biopic alleges, it's no surprise that they kept it close to their vests. It's not easy to do today, and we've had fifty years of sexual revolution and counter-revolution to pave the way.

What interests me most about the movie is the timing of its release, a moment so very reminiscent of the times in which his work attained its greatest notoriety.

Alfred Kinsey was lionized, but he was also roundly attacked, especially when he dared to show that women's sex lives were as diverse as men's. In the movie we meet Prok's hateful old fire-and-brimstone dad (who, in the end, appears to have a secret or two he wants to protect), and we meet Tim Curry as a disapprovingly nasty prude (whose casting is so postmodern, I almost squealed), an Indiana U colleague who's Kinsey's nemesis throughout. Senator Joe McCarthy himself has a brief role, too, as one of Kinsey's investigators. (Kinsey was one of the most widely snooped-on people ever, and even J. Edgar's boys couldn't dig up the dirt on him. Many of the anti-Kinsey screeds are made up, pure and simple.) But if the Kinsey Reports were going to be reprised today (for which there is no will in any research institute in the land; the idea of fighting for the funding alone exhausts researchers before they get the paperwork filled out), his nemeses would be sitting in the highest seats in government. Imagine Kinsey up against old breast-o-phobe John Ashcroft! Imagine the folks who have been working night and day to give us anti–same-sex marriage amendments and abstinence-only sex education!

All these folks are glad Kinsey is dead, and they want to keep him dead. Only trouble is, as far as they're concerned, he's not dead enough.

To the neoconservative fundamentalists and absexuals who continue to excoriate Kinsey and his work, the job is only half done. Basically, these folks want the land to go back to the days when fire and brimstone *meant* something. They don't *want* to live in a sexually pluralistic society. They don't *want* to be tempted by other people's choices. If repression is good enough for them (they reason), it's good enough for me…and for you too.

Kinsey may not have wanted to lead a revolution when he switched from gall wasps to sex histories. But his work kicked open a door that was only stuck shut. If you have picked up this book, you have reason to care about the state of the cultural changes he inspired. It's just shorthand, but none of us who's needed a sex question answered or found a place to have our desires met can afford to think our lives would be the same without Alfred Kinsey. And keep your eyes open, because we're living in a country where plenty of people would like to see him erased.

Superheroines in Trouble
Don Rasner

I've written for a lot of editors during my career. Most of them haven't taught me much, unless you count the control freak who drilled me on the exact rules of semicolon use.

One, though, did share with me a nugget of truth that I've never seen unproven. We were talking about the Internet and the amazing number of sex-related websites that seemed to spring up on it as soon as AOL burst onto the scene. During the conversation my editor said something like this: "Every new form of technology is inevitably used for pornography." To prove this, he pointed to the VCR, the amazing tool that allowed the horny toads of the world to watch smut films in the privacy of their own basements and bedrooms.

I was reminded of my editor's wise words one recent morning as I stared, blurry-eyed, at my computer screen. The little clock at its bottom said that it was 3:30 in the morning. But I wasn't ready to give up just yet. I desperately wanted to find one cartoon of a naked Laura Croft—probably getting violated by a man-eating plant, a well-hung cannibal, or a slobbering jungle tiger—that I hadn't seen before.

Sad to report, that night I had no luck. Not surprising, considering I've spent good chunks of my free time doing this same thing: scouring the back alleys of the Internet looking for comic book superheroines in big trouble, always of the sexual kind. Yep, I'm one of those freaks who are into a little something called superheroine-in-peril art.

If you're a person who gets your rocks off by thumbing through Victoria's Secret catalogs or *Playboy* magazine, what might surprise you most is that I'm not that unusual. A lot of people out there get their jollies by downloading cartoons of the Joker having his way with Batgirl. Don't believe me? Just log on to Yahoo Groups, and in that little bar where you can search for specific groups, type in the word *superheroine*. You'll turn up sites that aren't X-rated, of course, but you'll get quite a few that are dedicated to superheroines in big trouble—trouble of the sexual kind.

What is this genre of kink? It's pretty simple, actually. Guys who are into it (most of the fan base seems to be males) like to stare at X-rated cartoons showing supervillains—or monsters, space aliens, giant plants, robots, and the like—sexually assaulting superheroines. You can find such smut about any superheroine you can imagine: Supergirl, Jean Grey, Laura Croft (I know, technically, she's not a superheroine, but she's much-loved), Batgirl, Miss Fantastic, and, the most popular of all, Wonder Woman.

I shouldn't limit the genre to cartoons, either. A lot of people are into something called photo-manips, short for photo-manipulations. These are usually stills taken from mainstream porn videos that are given a superheroine touch through computer technology. For instance, the creator of a photo-manip may superimpose a fake of Wonder Woman's bustier and tiara to a screen capture of porn star Kira Kenner giving some unseemly porn stud a blow job. Plenty of companies are out there, too, selling superheroine videos for adults, mostly over the Internet. They usually feature women with dirty blonde hair, no acting talent, and a need for quick cash getting their leotards ripped off by other women with dirty blonde hair, no acting talent, and an equal need for quick cash. Want a story? Maybe a plot? Good luck.

I admit, of course, that even the superheroine stuff that I *do* like—the homemade comic strips, cartoons, and erotic fan fiction—isn't exactly high art, and I'd never admit to anyone that I was into this stuff, which is why I have a pseudonym. For one thing, it's incredibly sophomoric, not to mention horribly written. You enjoy typos and misspellings? Then read some of the work of the Internet's most prolific superheroine-in-peril artists; you'll get a whole slew of them. Even more disturbing, much of superheroine-in-peril art is vile. We're talking graphic depictions of rape here, and not only of the human-on-human kind. One of the first superheroine-in-peril online comics I found boasted a scene where a man-eating plant not only rapes a female jungle warrior, but also leaves her pregnant. The last panel shows the heroine clutching her already-bloated stomach and wailing, "Oh, God, I'm pregnant!" And that's actually a fairly tame scene for this genre. The heroines of some of the other comics I've seen have endured even worse fates. A comic featuring She-Ra from the old *He-Man* television series comes to mind. In this one an animated sword, after sexually assaulting She-Ra, hacks off her limbs one by one.

As a stripper, and a good-looking one, Taylor had seen plenty of guys like Dan O'Brian.

They'd hang around the club where she danced in sunny Tucson, eying her every gyration, and then approach her afterward. Some would want to date her, of course. Others offered her dubious-sounding offers to pose for adult movies or magazines.

But O'Brian pitched something different: He wanted to turn Taylor into a superheroine.

O'Brian was starting a business, one that would evolve into the website known as Superheroine Central (www.superheroinecentral.com). The site today is a busy one, filled with scores of women, both real and cartoon, wearing the skimpiest of superheroine costumes and inevitably falling prey to evil villains armed with chloroform. It, and a sister site devoted to the same type of thing in a science fiction setting (www.spacebabecentral.com), and a third devoted to more generic female fighting (www.catfightcentral.com) each generate about $40,000 a month in subscription revenue for O'Brian. The three sites together boast more than 1,800 members.

Back when Taylor first met him, though, O'Brian didn't seem much different than any of the other slightly creepy guys hanging around her club hoping to one day brag about "banging a stripper."

"He came in and asked me if I would be willing to pose for him as a superheroine," Taylor said. "I immediately said no. It sounded kind of strange. He came back the next week and asked me if I'd do it for five hundred dollars for a two-hour shoot. Hmmm, that made me think. That wasn't bad money. I asked him if my boyfriend could come along. He said sure, so I decided to go along. Of course, as soon as I got there, he noticed that I didn't have a boyfriend."

That day, three and a half years ago, Taylor became Ultra Woman. Of course, she didn't keep her tiny costume on for long, and soon she was portraying a series of hot, and quite beatable, superheroines for O'Brian in photo stories and miniature videos, giving bad guys ferocious karate chops, power-packed punches, and ironclad headlocks. Of course, the reason thousands logged on every week to see her, and the growing number of girls O'Brian added—girls who'd play characters named Power Gal, Ms. Freedom, and others—wasn't to see them dish out the hurting on villains. People paid to watch villains capture Taylor, rip off her costume, tie her up, and have their way with her.

Taylor has since graduated from these appearances, and now works as O'Brian's personal assistant at his growing business. But she has no regrets about her time as Ultra Woman.

"I have to say, this has been the most fun I've ever had," Taylor reported. "The people here are good. It's more like a family atmosphere than anything else. And I've had the chance to do some creative things. I'd do it again in a second."

O'Brian is an unlikely leader in the superheroine-in-peril community. For one thing, he considers himself a Republican. Secondly, he once served in the U.S. Air Force. He's also no comic book geek; he has plenty of other hobbies and interests. He's a student of Arabic languages, for instance.

But like many folks making money in this industry, O'Brian traces his involvement in it back to his days as a horny twelve-year-old wishing tragedy on the world's most famous Amazonian queen.

"I remember reading Wonder Woman's comic books. There'd be this monster crushing her, and I'm sitting there thinking, 'Am I supposed to be worried about her?' I wanted to be the monster. I guess it's that combination of sex and violence. That's one of the more objectionable fantasies to have these days, but it is there. It's undeniable," O'Brian said.

★　★　★

Yes, violence. Now there's the tricky part of this whole thing. These days most any fetish is OK, no matter how strange. But if that fetish happens to include violence? Well, that's a whole different story.

The same violence inherent in the superheroine-in-peril genre that attracts subscribers to places like Superheroine Central also makes the fetish one that its fans keep quiet about. Its creators, too, like to keep out of public sight. Dan O'Brian is in fact a pseudonym. Other leading practitioners of the genre include people who call themselves Villain, Mr. X, and Nightwing 316.

As an example of why people who fuel this fetish keep their real names secret, just take a look at Mr. X. He's one of the most skillful users of a computer program called Poser, which allows him to create realistic 3-D comic strips. His heroines, inevitably busty, feature realistic skin tones, flowing hair, and an endless array of facial expressions. They also have incredibly bad luck, sexually speaking. And it's this "bad luck" that keeps artists like Mr. X, who are actually quite good at what they do, from wanting to take any public credit for their work.

One of Mr. X's most popular heroines is Ms. Americana, a type of clueless Wonder Woman. Dressed in the skimpiest red-white-and-blue costume possible, Ms. Americana blunders into one humiliating misadventure after another. In one strip, which can be found at a special section on Superheroine Central reserved for Mr. X's work, Ms. Americana is repeatedly gang-raped by both a gang of thugs and a high-tech machine called the Rape-O-Matic. In another strip, a painful-looking machine squeezes milk out of her massive breasts while a group of villains looks on laughing. But have no fear, in both strips Ms. Americana wins at the end, turning the tables on her tormentors at the last possible moment.

Mr. X has been creating this sort of art for twenty-five years.

But with the Internet, he's been able to find a huge audience. Unlike O'Brian, he draws and experiments with Poser strictly for enjoyment. Mr. X's site at Superheroine Central is free to all visitors. He's not uncomfortable with the violence in his strips, seeing it as a release for men who are tired of being on the receiving end—at least in the nation's comic strips and action movies—of a series of body blows, nose-bloodying punches, and knees to the groin.

"This is going to sound harsh, but the more men with low self-esteem out there, the bigger the customer base for us," Mr. X said in an email interview. "I think the current PC feminist climate has helped a great deal in providing a huge customer base. Basically, TV is a lot more taunting and hostile now than it was in the Batgirl/Wonder Woman days. It's a lot more unfriendly to men. Men are constantly criticized."

Fellow superheroine-in-peril artist Villain, who operates Superheroines' Demise (www.sooperhero.com), has run his site as a pay site since 1998. He won't divulge how much money he makes from it, but he does say that membership has been steadily growing. He says he had no idea how popular his work would become when he started Superheroines' Demise seven years ago. Looking back now, though, he says, it's easy to understand what attracts fans to this genre: He and other artists give comic-book fans, mostly male, exactly what they've always wanted but have never been able to get from such mainstream publishers as Marvel and D.C.

"Let me ask you a question: If you were a diabolical, twisted maniac supervillain hell-bent on destruction, anarchy, chaos, and evil, then what do you think you would do if you had one of these costumed crime-fighting babes tied up in your lair? Explain to them your plot to blow up the world and then bid them adieu as the bomb you strapped to their feet slowly ticks away? Hell no, man! You would, at the very, very least, take a peek underneath to see what has been trying to ooze out of that tight spandex costume for the last 1,000 issues on the newsstand,"Villain said.

Finding actresses for the genre's movies isn't always easy. O'Brian, not surprisingly, struggles to find women willing to play characters who are raped or beaten. Because of this, he sometimes finds actresses who cannot, in the least bit, act. Other times he lands a coup, and manages to attract a semifamous actress to his site. But often the minor celebrity will require that O'Brian tone down his act a bit. His site once featured a former Penthouse Pet, for example. She was willing to wear a sexy costume and show lots of skin. But she wasn't willing to do much else, so O'Brian had to be creative with the script and narrative for his movie.

Other models, though, have no qualms about participating in the genre. There's Leslie Culton, for one, a B-movie actress who has also run a busy side career posing as various superheroines, everyone from Vampirella to Wonder Woman. Her online Yahoo fan club has 1,300 members.

She recently appeared in a photo comic for O'Brian's site as Ms. Freedom. Pouring her ample curves into her red-white-and-blue costume, Culton looks both girl-next-door-ish and incredibly hot. She also gets the living crap beat out of her.

Culton, though, doesn't see the genre as a negative thing. Instead, she says, it gives males a chance to live out their darkest fantasies without actually causing harm to any real, living people.

"This appeals to the naughty, evil side of men," Culton said about the genre,"the part of them that twists their inner mustaches in wicked delight at the damsel tied to the railroad track. I am sure there were all kinds of little boys who wanted to be the villain taking Wonder Woman prisoner. Now the little boys are big boys, and they want to see what is underneath the costumes."

Boogie Dykes
Michelle Tea

The murmur of gossip and opinion in my living room just barely drowns out the gurgles, moans, and cries of "yeah...fuck me!!!!" that stream from the collagen-plump lips of porn stars cavorting on my TV screen. I don't normally entertain guests with videos rented from Tenderloin smut shops, but then my guests normally aren't award-winning pornographers like Shar Rednour and Jackie Strano.

Through their two-person video production team, S.I.R. (Sex, Indulgence, and Rock 'n' roll), respected Bay Area sex educators Rednour and Strano have created fierce, realistic, playful, and downright glamorous sex-education and erotica videos for the past several years. A classic is *Bend Over Boyfriend,* featuring Dr. Carol Queen—a postmodern Dr. Ruth—teaching women how to penetrate their male partners safely and sensitively. Strano, with her all-dyke rock band the Hail Marys, is also a much loved performer in the queer community. Known more for their pro-feminist, pro-sex politics than for pornography, Rednour and Strano are possibly the first members of San Francisco's dyke underground to bring real lesbian sex into the porn mainstream.

S.I.R. is also best known for releasing the most luscious bit of dyke pornography ever to wet a girl's panties: the double feature *Hard Love/How to Fuck in High Heels*. And out of the 11,000-plus adult videos released each year—videos produced in enormous, wealthy complexes in the San Fernando Valley, with budgets to rival 20th Century Fox's—*Hard Love* was selected by the respected *Adult Video News* magazine (porn's version of *Variety*) as a nominee in the categories Best All-Girl Feature and Best All-Girl Scene. Rednour and Strano would be honored guests at the porn industry's gala event, the AVN Awards, held annually in—where else?—Las Vegas.

In the days leading up to the awards ceremony, we still couldn't believe what was happening. Dykes account for less than 1 percent of the more than 700 million porn movies rented in the past year, and the percentage of dykes actually making porn is doubtless smaller. We huddled around my VCR, trying to figure it out. The blue movies flickering across my TV screen were some of the films the pair was up against, and watching them fueled my amazement: How did a couple of freaky, sex-radical dykes capture the respect of an industry whose business is manufacturing exaggerated clichés of female sexuality?

S.I.R. is a classic do-it-yourself operation. Dynamic couple Rednour and Strano not only wrote, cast, directed, and starred in their video but were also responsible for its distribution nation-wide. *Hard Love* features Strano and C. C. Belle as newly broken-up lovers who fuck around with some chicks, have a big-ass lesbian process about it, then fuck their brains out. *How to Fuck in*

High Heels is a glittery, candy-colored rock video with femme diva Rednour demonstrating on a team of hotties how to properly strap it on while buckled into a pair of platforms.

Made by dykes, for dykes, the video features real, local dykes fucking the way real dykes fuck—these are not career porn actresses with skinny, unadorned bodies and silicone tits. The only silicone in *Hard Love* is the stuff strapped between the girls' legs, and even in this *Hard Love* differs from the mainstream. Big-budget pornos generally employ low-budget sex toys, the plasticky, weird stuff found in porn stores throughout the USA, not the quality sex accessories found in women-centric shops like Good Vibrations and used in most dykes' bedrooms.

If you used mainstream porn as a guide to real lesbian sex, you'd think that women enjoy being sloppily stabbed in the cunt by a jabbing tongue, spend hours in the 69 position, or have long, gently sensuous make-out sessions that ended with lots of showy tongue-touching. The girls in S.I.R.'s video fuck hard. Like real dykes, they have embarrassing process sessions with their exes; then they have conflicted, complicated, and raw fuck sessions.

But probably the most important and obvious difference between *Hard Love* and any other "girl-girl" video on the market is that *Hard Love* shows butch dykes—a lesbian reality the man-made flicks unsurprisingly ignore. For Rednour and Strano—a femme–butch couple who have been involved in the specifically Bay Area sex-radical and sex-education scene that brought us Susie Bright, the San Francisco Sex Information hotline, and Good Vibrations—showing butch dykes having hot sex was both essentially authentic and politically crucial.

In the summer of its release, *Hard Love/How to Fuck in High Heels* premiered around the world at lesbian and gay film festivals, winning the hearts of queer girls starved for girl-girl porn featuring actual dykes they'd want to fuck, not porn-industry Barbies bent into "lesbian" positions.

That the film was a queer smash is unsurprising. That it was nominated by the big players is shocking. And there I was on the way to the AVN Awards to see it all happen.

"I think AVN is pushing the envelope by nominating us," Rednour says. "It's them being a little political, and that's cool. It might be a diversity move. They could be so sick of seeing the same ol' stuff. But it would be a miracle if we won." Strano is more optimistic. "We have a lot of competition," she agrees. "But we have a chance at getting Best All-Girl Feature, because we have real dykes."

That's the truth. To cast *Hard Love/High Heels,* the pair posted "Actresses Wanted" flyers at San Francisco's sapphic watering holes, and the girls who showed up to audition were housepainters, sex toy salespeople, bartenders, social workers, and strippers—good old-fashioned dyke occupations.

"Our thing is turning everyday people into sex stars, through fantasy and dirty talk," Rednour says. "People with sexy attitudes, friendly personalities, a sense of adventure and exhibitionism. The really funny thing was finding a butch bottom who would take her clothes off on-screen." Though the presence of butch dykes in the video may shake shit up in the porn industry, it's possibly just as radical for San Francisco's dyke community. Butches are supposed to be the silent, nonglamorous types, while their femme counterparts get all the eroticizing attention. As a result, butch tit-baring is rare here—butch boobs are more likely to be found strapped beneath sports bras and Ace bandages than bared for a camera.

"We really had an agenda of eroticizing butch women, and part of that is not hiding the butches' chests," Strano says. "A lot of us don't like to talk about [our breasts] or deal with them. But we're women, and our femme girlfriends love our tits and don't want us to cut them off and turn into men."

San Francisco is known throughout queer USA as a hotbed of foxy butches. No other city allows girls who don't feel girly the freedom to crack open their psyches and draw out their inner cowboy, leatherman, hesher dude, or nerd boy, while still finding employment, let alone safety. In a place where butchness is sexy and revered, it often feels like the butchest girls win. The reality of womanly curves and soft flesh can feel like betrayals to dykes cultivating a tough machismo. But the point of butch-femme sex, as portrayed in Rednour and Strano's video, is that what's essentially hot about butches, and what is often absurdly forgotten, even by dykes, is that they are women—women who can wear masculinity better than men.

Since sometimes it seems like it's easier for butch girls to become transmen than to confront any ambivalence they feel for their bodies, this was quite a challenging agenda. Of all the swaggering boy-girls in town, only two butch dykes auditioned. And even they weren't itching to fling off their tops. "It was a process," admits Johnny Fremont, who was required to perform one of those rarely seen butch stripteases for *Hard Love*. "I didn't want to. But I knew where they were coming from and why it's important to show butch tits, 'cause butches have such body issues. It was hard, but I'm glad I did it."

"My personal agenda was, 'Check it out: butches have hot sex,' " Strano says. "Lesbians have really hot sex. It is nothing like you imagine. It is not 'girl-on-girl.' People think we're freaks of nature, that we lead lonely lives, and the truth is, people wish they had our lives."

★　★　★

Cruising into the desert wonderland of Las Vegas, where the couple lodge in a very *Boogie Nights*–ish hotel equipped with mirrored ceilings and a sunken hot tub beside the enormous bed, you could agree that yes, most people would not kick such a life out of their bed.

Along for the awards is Josephine X, the corkscrew-curled starlette of *How to Fuck in High Heels.* Introduced to porn through a college research paper, Josephine "thought it was totally hot to learn that women watched pornography, and liked it, and wanted to be in it. I started reading a lot of books, people like Susie Bright and Annie Sprinkle, watching a lot of porn, and educating myself. I think that planted a seed."

Rednour credits her working-class, religious upbringing for her desire to bring quality dyke porn to the masses. "My parents had a healthy sex life," she says. "You worked at the factory, came home, ate dinner, watched a little TV, went to bed, and fucked each night. I'm coming with that as a background, that sex is a respected part of love and intimacy." And the mania Rednour once used in her work as a teenage minister in the Midwest paved the way for her transformation into a queer sex radical who just can't stop evangelizing. "When you're like me, with a Christian background and obsessive, you have to do everything to the 10th degree," she says. "It's not enough for me to have great sex. I want everyone to have great sex!"

Strano also sees her place in the porn world as essentially humanitarian. She wants "to make the world a better place by showing people that sex is good, sex is fun, people should have more of it, and the best that they can."

It's the night of the awards ceremony, and the S.I.R. posse is navigating the slot-machine labyrinth of the Venetian casino. The femmes are shimmering like disco balls, the butches tucked proudly into suits. The pack's visible queerness, plus the abundance of tattoos and unnaturally colored hair and absence of silicone, jarringly separates us from the throngs of mainstream porn icons heading into the ballroom.

A line of camera-toting men, press and porn fans, pop their flashbulbs in our faces and loom over us with camcorders. In a different situation such attention could summon a panic attack, but we all cruise by, freaky and fabulous. How strange, to have a portion of America prone to treating me and my kind like a bunch of drug-addicted no-good hooligans, gasping and snapping pictures like we're royalty.

It's a shallow delight, but I revel in it. It feels like the biggest scam in the world that this ragtag band of queer misfits are honored guests at such a prestigious event, the fringe of the fringe.

The ballroom is enormous and dark, with electric green laser lights shooting through the air. The baroque grandeur of the Venetian is teeming with women sewed into eensy scraps of expensive rhinestone and sequins, dresses with backs that plunge practically to asscrack, and tops that veer into silicone caverns. This is the Academy Awards for starlettes whose roles normally don't require much costume and don't usually garner them much respect or acclaim.

Most of the women parading around effortlessly on their tottering heels spent all day having their hair curled and pinned into cascading swoops; their faces glitter with professionally applied makeup. The buffet tables are loaded with seafood that's been shipped into this landlocked palace, and quiet waiters scurry about balancing trays heavy with tiny, elegant snacks. I notice with a bit of a thrill that we've been seated with Chloe Nicholle, the porn world's Julianne Moore—an award-winning big-time player, but unexpectedly so considering her small breasts, cinnamon hair, and fondness for kink. She's indie enough that she lent her talent to one of S.I.R.'s first videos, *Bend Over Boyfriend 2,* a blend of sex ed and smut geared toward hetero couples looking to explore boy booty.

"I love Shar, and I love Jackie," Chloe enthuses. The combination of her tough voice, princessy prettiness, and that I just watched her get massively fucked on TV the other night makes me very nervous. "Anytime I can help out women who want to direct, good, I'll do it!" Chloe says. "I'm always the girl who's getting it up the butt, and to be able to put on a strap-on and do a guy up the butt [in *Bend Over Boyfriend 2*]—that appealed to me."

Like other industry insiders I've spoken to, Chloe is not surprised by S.I.R.'s nomination. "It stood out," she says. "It's a good product, and it shows. And they're going to be nominated and recognized for that. You can be nobody out there, and if you make a good product with your camcorder, and you want to retail it—if we like it, it's going to get noticed."

The award show begins. Jenna Jameson, the event's MC, is unfortunately everything you'd fear a big blonde porn star would be. She can barely make it through her hokey prescripted jokes ("Let's hope that Bush isn't too hard on the pussy!"). Some established players are brought up to present awards—a weirdly charismatic Ron Jeremy, the predictably offensive Al Goldstein.

When pink-haired Cindy of *Big, Beautiful Girls* and tiny specialty-video starlette Bridgette Powers take the stage, the cameramen ignore them and fill the video screen with shots of modelesque audience members, as if hours upon hours of identical, skinny, tanned girls hadn't been enough. I perk up when it's time for Best All-Girl Scene, preparing to pound on my table and hoot and holler. But the presenter doesn't even mention *Hard Love.*

I sip my cocktail with bitter dejection. No one thought our

underdog friends would win, but we at least wanted the opportunity to root for them. I'm itching for this thing to end so I can hit some nickel slots and slurp free casino cocktails. It's hard for anyone to pay attention to the tedium on the stage; the night has gone on too long.

Which is why no one notices when the blonde onstage announces Best All-Girl Feature: *Hard Love/How to Fuck in High Heels!* I almost fall out of my chair trying to get Rednour's and Strano's attention. They're chatting and fiddling with the free lube packages bouqueted on each table.

"You won!" I shriek. People rush over to our table screaming the same thing. Josie X and Johnny Fremont hug each other off the floor, Rednour and Strano are making out ecstatically. "Oh my god," they chant, bewildered. I get chills. Our table is now engulfed by congratulators making the filmmakers the stunned and smiling centerpieces.

On the van ride home, Rednour indulges us with a fantasy of Dyke Mainstreet USA, where the couple will be greeted by a marching band and a ticker-tape parade. "This is bringing home the prize for all the dykes," she says, beaming. "Not just San Francisco but everywhere."

"I get so high off my work," Rednour says. "And it's great to be able to share that work with Jackie, who gets me off in every other way, too."

Sex Machines
Timothy Archibald

When I ring the doorbell at Spindoll Manufacturing and Sales, Inc., in Henderson, Nevada, Rick and Kristy are just waking up. There on the same block as The Red Rooster, a long-standing swing club nestled in an industrial park, the couple creates, builds, and sells sex machines in a warehouse-cum-storefront shop. They open their showroom for tryouts and demonstrations from 9 P.M. to 3 A.M., six days a week.

The walls of the shop are painted pink with baby-blue trim. Even though this is our first meeting in person, Rick greets me as a friend, and leads me through a door into a giant warehouse space filled with lathes, band saws, industrial equipment, and an area filled with weight-lifting equipment. He leads me into a giant RV parked and tethered to the wiring in the warehouse. Rick and Kristy are cooking a breakfast of eggs, bacon, and coffee. I help myself to some strong coffee from the Mr. Coffee maker, and we talk. These two are funny, good conversationalists, easy-going, and they never ask me why I want to interview them and take photographs of their sex machines.

I learn that Rick is a former massage therapist, a part-time Internet porn actor, and—to me—an inspired inventor. He conceived of three inventions during a time in his life when he was trying to get out of the massage business: an indestructible steel mailbox, a bed to be used for filming home pornography, and a sex machine he calls the Orgasmo. The mailbox was too expensive to build, the bed was too cumbersome, but the Orgasmo quickly became a sought-after commodity. More popular with pornography makers and sex clubs than individuals, the machine made Spindoll famous in the world of sex machines.

We talk, and I take photographs, as we move around the machine shop, and I take in the creators and birthplace of the highest-priced sex machine on the market, selling for $5,535. The Orgasmo is beautifully crafted from steel and has a platform of four legs that move along on wheels. The legs support a steel neck and a large steel box, out of which comes the thrusting shaft. It looks like a tank of sorts, or some type of rocket launcher, stronger and heavier than it may need to be. It is short and muscular, reflecting the stature of its creator, who is also an avid bodybuilder.

Rick is proud of his machine. "I've made the ultimate sex machine.... My machine will make more women come faster, harder, and just get them off better than anyone else's machines, no question. It does everything you want it to do: It angles, it raises, it lowers, it vibrates, it thrusts, it's fast, it's slow. Shit, it does everything but snuggle with you."

A preacher's daughter born in Kentucky, Kristy met Rick when she applied for a job to become his secretary; now they run Spindoll together. As I follow them around the shop, peppering them with my questions and taking photographs, I see Post-it notes reading "I love you" on computer monitors, and snapshots of them together dot the entire work area. For extra money, Kristy also works as a masseuse at the local nudist camp. She openly tells me about her relationship with sex and her relationship with Rick. "I don't really get the swinging thing. Rick is a swinger and it's something I need to respect, but it's not something that's for me.... And then these machines—I'm not into them. I like the real thing: squeezing, hugging, cuddling, just holding each other. It was hard enough for me to get comfortable selling someone a dildo."

I spend the entire day documenting the couple, and into the evening, and soon after dinner they'll need to open their storefront. Kristy tells me, "When we opened up the shop and hung out the sign that said 'Unique Sex Toys, Free Demos,' Rick and I agreed that I'd do the demos on the men, and he would do the demos on the women. We'd keep it polite and professional, always courteous. The first guy I did was a stoned drunken pervert! I was giving him a demo of the Fucksall (a reciprocating electric saw with dildo adapted to the end) on our demonstration bed and he kept asking me to touch him. Here I am ramming the Fucksall up his ass and he wants me to touch him! I got out of it by explaining to him that it would be unsafe for me to operate the Fucksall without both hands on the machine—we have regulations we need to follow! At the end, he was climaxing like he was having a convulsion or something. I just ran out of the room. He went into the restroom, cleaned himself up, and then said he'd be ready in a few minutes for another demo.

"I had to say, 'Sorry, sir, just one demo per person per night, and we are closed.' "

★ ★ ★

On my way back to my hotel, I remembered the first time I saw a sex machine. While researching a story about independent garage inventors, I came across an MSN group called Sex Machine Inventors, a small Web community for inventors of sex machines. And it was a community scattered across the entire United States, nestled in some of the most unlikely, head-scratching communities and neighborhoods for a niche—even fetish—sexual subculture. But I was less surprised by the existence of the subculture than startled by the amateur photographs of the machines themselves—as a professional photojournalist, I felt envious of those who shot the amateur snaps of the inventors' machines in their cluttered domestic rooms. The photos were startlingly perfect to me as art—honest, innocent, and unpretentious documents of fascinating creations. The inventors had unwittingly created the type of photographs I've tried all my life to create: photographs that were of simply fascinating subject matter, but also reflecting with pride, fascination, and a bit of reluctant humor.

I began my obsession with documenting this subculture by endeavoring to meet Peter Rodgers and Tony Pirelli of Cybernet Entertainment, the men behind the infamous sex machine website called FuckingMachines.com. Both Tony and Peter graciously scheduled times to meet with me and endure my questions, when no one was filming men and women having sex with machines. I was stunned when I first entered their studio complex in Northern California—I had assumed this was a small venture on the part of two amateur, start-up entrepreneurs. An elevator took me up to a polished, wood-floored office space filled with people busily working on computers, editing films, and doing office work suitable to a large company. As we talked, Tony led me to his office, with a door in the back opening up to a series of studios with different themes: a schoolroom, a doctor's office, a living room,

and more. All porn film clichés, true, but the sets seemed to be
executed to the highest Hollywood standards. I discovered both
Tony and Peter to be articulate, cultured, and savvy.

Peter and Tony agreed to introduce me to the inventors who
made many of their machines, sex machine creators who were
scattered across America in tiny towns. Even though I had already
made a reputable connection with FuckingMachines.com, I discovered the sex machine community to be an undeclared sexual
underground. I spent a lot of time on machine-oriented online
Listserves, such as "machinesex" and "homemadebdsmequip-
ment" at YahooGroups.com, and at "milkingmenbymachines" at
MSN.com. I only approached the people who seemed most forthcoming and involved in the idea of making their machines, and
talking about them. It was essential to stage my communication to
establish trust: I'd begin a dialogue via email, talk with the inventors on the phone, then schedule a time to go visit them in their
workplace—typically their garage, laundry room, or extra guest
room. Whom I chose to visit greatly depended on who seemed the
most passionate about what they were doing: inventors who really
felt they were on a mission, and were proud of what they do. It
didn't matter to me who was popular, or who was making money.
I was only interested in their passion for the sex machine.

The first in-the-field, at-home sex machine inventor I met was
Paul Sartan, of Sartan's Workshop in Redwood City, California.
Paul was patient and forthcoming in his email responses to me,
and then on the phone, and when we met he went out of his
way to make me comfortable asking questions, even though I had
concerns about the ominous business name. Was it supposed to be
Santa's Workshop? Satan's? Sartan's website proclaims that they are
"committed to advancing the art of sex machines." But I discovered that the manufacturing site was actually Paul's home, shared

with his wife and kids in a conservative suburb. He had happily agreed to spend time with me, but we had to be done by the time his kids were home from school. On walking in, I found the place cluttered with the kids' bikes, and hedge trimmers tossed in around the band saw and drill press.

Paul wore a T-shirt with his favorite basketball team on it, and had an almost teacher-like air about him, seemingly open to all the naïve questions I asked, all while exuding a casual humor about the subject matter at hand—making machines for people to have sex with. We hung out in his garage and his kitchen, surrounded by domestic items he has turned into machines; he made me coffee and we sipped, talked, looked at machines, and I took photographs. On occasion, he would leave me alone with the machines while he attended to machine-related business on the phone or computer. I shot a pasta maker chassis he'd found at a thrift store and had transformed into a sex machine: a dusty prototype spanking machine that sat on a shelf in his workspace. He returned to display a four-person sex machine for me on his pool table in the family room.

Paul told me, "I think it is a very common fantasy, this machine fucking fantasy thing. It really comes down to the desire to have something that can out-perform a man. This machine doesn't get tired and can maintain 250 thrusts per minute. I mean, even on my best day I could maybe do 150, and not for long."

With Paul, his "shop" was really integrated into his home—things were always put away when the kids got home. He used the garage, a spare room, and a shed in the back for sex machine work purposes, sharing the space with his wife's stained glass work area. Though initially secretive about his business with the neighbors, he had made Sartan's Workshop a part of their neighborhood community. Paul and his wife, Jenn, have formed a fast friendship with their neighbor Stephanie. Stephanie at first seemed to be disgusted by the machines—then became fascinated by them. Now she has begun dating the machinist who makes Paul's more complex metal parts.

When the kids did come home at 5 P.M., I put away my cameras and equipment, and Paul and his wife and I retired to the backyard to drink beer and discuss sex machines while the kids played in their rooms. Paul's kids seemed oblivious to the mechanical parts around the garage. Without a dildo, the way Paul sells them, the machines look surprisingly innocuous. They could be anything, like possibly something to pump up a bike tire with.

Steve Ryan lets me into his home off the highway in south Kansas City, Kansas. It is empty, a big house nicely decorated in Ethan Allen style furniture. The rec room is a classic bachelor pad: a sunken bar, big decorative wall sculptures of a reclining female form, and a sex swing set up in the back. I note the photographic lights and tripods in the room, easily accessible if needed to photograph something. A neon bar sign, a wall-mounted TV. Pinkish walls with black leather couches. This is where Steve and his current roommate, Cassie, are planning to shoot and launch a sex machine website called "Cassie's Dollhouse."

Steve is in his forties, with a flat stomach that he tells me is in shape from swimming. I notice right away that he has a friendly "everyman's" face, not what someone would describe as handsome, but with a nice, open smile. Steve described himself to me in his emails as a voyeur. He came to my attention because he was posting images on a machine-oriented Listserv that had developed an enormous following. People became members of this Listserv just to see his images. His work had an unusual intimacy, an unusual familiarity between subject and camera, a relationship that viewers really responded to.

Currently single, Steve has lived through two marriages and divorces in this home. His current housemate, Cassie, is an eighteen-year-old community college student whom Steve has known for a few months. Cassie and Steve tell me about "Cassie's Dollhouse." Their plan is to use Cassie and her friends as talent, and Steve's classically decorated home as the set. Steve explains how this all got started. "I ran an ad in the local newspaper that read, 'Voyeur seeking sexually adventurous beautiful females with excellent bodies and excellent attitudes to audition with simulated sexual machines. Up to $200 per session. Please call: 949-668-XXXX.'"

Steve explained to the women who answered the ad that he had sex machines that he'd bought for an ex-girlfriend but that were at home just collecting dust. Stating that he was a voyeur, he'd tell them that, frankly, he just wanted someone to come over and play on them while he videotaped them. It began as a private sexual endeavor, only for his own viewing, with no intention of putting together a website. He told me, "The first ad, I got a huge response from because no one knew what the hell I was talking about! I would meet with them at a restaurant. If I thought they were worthy, they looked nice, they looked good in clothes, then the next thing was 'Come on over to my house, drop your linen, start your grinnin'.' I met a lot of nice girls that way. At my age, age forty-five, these nineteen-year-olds are what I'm attracted to, and these girls are not going to be attracted to me, so I gotta have a hook. Something to make them comfortable coming over. The machines are that hook."

Steve offers up to $200 per session because "You're not going to get girls to come over just for fun and games…. Oh sure, there's drama. The last thing I need in my life is drama, and hanging around with nineteen-year-old girls gets you that, but it's a trade-off. It's a hell of a lot better than hanging around with a forty-five-year-old wife you never talk to and never want to have sex with. How many guys wanna be Hugh Hefner? I don't have the money Hefner has, nor the empire, nor the means in which to have lots and lots of women at any given time. But I've created an atmosphere that simulates that on a smaller scale. I knock on wood a hundred times a day—I'm very thankful. That's why I film it all, 'cause things could change and I may never see that girl again."

We go to lunch in rainy downtown Kansas City and continue the interview, and Steve invites me to stay and photograph the audition that he and Cassie have planned with a model that evening. That night, Adrianne comes to the house and casually greets Steve and Cassie, both of whom will do the filming. They had all met once before at a restaurant to allow everyone to get to know each other on neutral territory. Here they meet for the second time, all in the rec room of Steve's house. Adrianne is getting $200 for the evening's work, and I get the sense that she just wants to do her audition, thank everyone for their time, get her money, and get on with the rest of her evening. But this "studio" is now her fake home, complete with a ringing phone, popcorn in the microwave, a football game on TV in the next room, and me, a photojournalist, hanging around watching. While setting up, Cassie and Steve nitpick each other on little details like the cameras and video gear.

Adrianne seems to be uncomfortable. *I* am uncomfortable. Cassie picks up on my unease and asks me, "How uncomfortable are you with everything that is going on right now? We don't really have a lot of boundaries in this house, and I know it makes some people uncomfortable." I thank her for picking up on my awkwardness, and admit that the situation makes me a bit nervous. then decide to try to maintain a professional stance and just let them be themselves.

Adrienne attempts to get positioned on the leather sofa with a sex machine called "One Der Woman." The machine is flat black, with a series of mechanical gears and exposed shafts and a red dildo at the end. She is having a difficult time with the machine—Cassie is on the phone with a friend and not able to help, while Steve is chatting to me about camera stuff. Adrianne explains that she can't get comfortable without some silence and guidance, and needs to concentrate to make everything work. Steve adjusts the machine to accommodate her, and hands her the controls. She finally guides the dildo into her vagina and allows the machine to penetrate her repeatedly, putting on a show that looks as if she's approaching orgasm.

As the motor warms up and the room is filled with the smooth, mechanical rhythm of the machine's flywheel turning, Steve can't seem to keep himself from flirting with Adrienne, telling her, "You know, honey, I have a nine-inch cock." Adrienne smiles back, keeping a professional balance between the sexual tension with Steve and completing the shoot. Steve seems disappointed by her requests for more money for every machine used, and every hour of her time spent. Afterward, everyone retires to the kitchen for a drink, with Adrienne casually sitting naked on the counter while she sips and the rest of us begin to clear the equipment, fully clothed. Adrienne tells Steve that she did not have an orgasm, but did enjoy the machine.

In the final result I see that evening, the videography and photography is raw and unpolished, with harsh lighting and white pops of on-camera flash. Typically, the defining quality of Steve's filming is the extreme acceptance and connection the girls emulate for him on camera. They seem to be performing for a friend, and to honestly connect with him. Steve knows the footage from tonight isn't going to be what he wants. "Look," he tells me after

Adrienne has left, "you need to want to hang out with us for this to work. That girl was all business. She didn't really like us. This is the problem with trying to make this a business. If it's not fun, it's going to show. I got a job, I don't need another one. But if I can make this work out with Cassie and her friends, to where it's fun, I will. I just don't know if it's gonna work."

Scott Ehalt and his dad, Cy, were searching for an extension cord as his newest sex machine sat on the kitchen table in their Champlin, Minnesota, home that doubles as the laboratory for Scott's company, Sex Machines Unlimited. At first glance Scott is the quintessential icon of an American outlaw biker: easily six feet tall, in a leather jacket and a Sturgis T-shirt, wearing a goatee and long hair. When he opens his mouth I can tell that his brain is running on overdrive; he is very focused, and likes to talk a lot, all the time. He speaks in run-on sentences, so many ideas and stories, one topic leading to another topic, stories tumbling out in a way that single story lines are hard to follow. Everything in his house is immaculate, each room neat as a pin.

The Pile Driver, Scott's first machine, was originally conceived for use at stag parties hosted by his motorcycle club. Tapping his skills as a customized motorcycle builder, Scott began Sex Machines Unlimited and has named his newest machine The Ultimate Ride.

The Ultimate Ride is a made of multicolored, powder-coated metal and Plexiglas. With the bright purple, orange, and yellow colors, it resembles an overlarge toy for a child. Scott's first machine, The Pile Driver, is much less refined: two 2-foot slabs of rough-cut steel act as supports to the motor and arm mechanism. An oversized dildo that belonged to his motorcycle group's clubhouse, nicknamed "Meatloaf," is supported on the moving bar of the machine. It took two people to move the machine. The new machine, The Ultimate Ride, was created after The Pile Driver was critiqued as being "too frightening to women." Scott's response was to create something "flashy and not intimidating." The machine mostly illustrates his tastes for motorcycle customizing.

Scott and I drive across town to get The Pile Driver out of a friend's garage. It's unclear to me why the friend had it, though I understand that the friend is a married guy, in a middle class suburb, with two kids. The machine is being stored in the garage with a snowmobile. Scott chain-smokes as he drives and tells me, "I always felt good about building things. I think I got it from my dad. It started with Legos, then Lincoln Logs, then it got real with the Erector Set. I've built houses, I've built machines, but I've never built a business...the learning curve is steep! We were planning a spam mail campaign of 20 million spam email addresses, but unfortunately the spammer ended up in prison."

Scott ponders his machines' target markets, explaining, "I'm not bisexual in any way, shape, or form. I'm strictly about the pussy. But this machine is good for any person I can think of. Gay men, gay closest cases, couples who aren't having sex, couples enhancing their sex life. And then there is the whole therapeutic aspect of it—we are trying to get it clinically tested at the medical school later this month. Renting it out to the women's prison is another idea I was thinking of. Why can't we do that?"

On a gray, humid day in Texas, I find Marlon Reynolds's apartment located in a high-end, gated complex in Austin. Marlon lets me into his crisp, air-conditioned apartment and places his prototype machine onto a flowered couch that dominates the small living room. He begins to tell me about himself, about the toys on the floor that belong to his son, and about the boy's mother with whom he shares custody. I sit in the living room, watching him set up his machine on the couch, trying to find a simple human element to include in my photograph—I guess the couch will be that element. He apologizes about the couch; he had simply borrowed it from a friend. He has agreed to my interviewing him and taking photographs of the machine, but nothing more, especially shots of him.

Marlon cuts an impressive figure; he is a muscular man in his late forties, smart and analytical, businesslike and serious. With Marlon it is all business. I set up my camera and he begins talking to me, my tape recorder running as I fiddle with the camera. He had sent the message that this was to be all business, nothing erotic or even nonclinical was to be discussed or, likely, permitted. It's as if we are discussing the pros and cons of an automobile he's trying to sell me, and he wants to discuss its functions in detail. Working as an engineer in the aluminum industry, Marlon had invented a dielectrically insulated, pneumatically operated robotic pipe cleaner, and a linear centrifuge. Currently working in the Texas real estate market, he spends his downtime engineering a digitally driven sex machine.

His next machine will be run by computer. The machine he shows me on the couch is only the analog version of this future machine. The arms were crafted from a drummer's cymbal stand; the body came from a chunk of PVC piping. It is unimpressive in structure, yet Marlon's machine is the only one designed to provide a variety in the pattern of thrust. The machine has a camshaft system of motion that provides a repeating, yet varied, pattern of thrusts. When completed, the machine's software driver will provide the same repeating yet varied combination of thrusts through digital programming, rather than mechanical cams or gears.

Marlon surveys his machine and explains, "I suspect this will be a new paradigm. The first test subject who tried the analog machine was visibly reduced to tears [from her orgasm]. The digital variant of my current machine will allow the customer to download a variety of WAV files from the Internet, burn them to a CD, and then essentially play the WAV files on their machine, in up to forty-five-minute increments. The WAV files will contain the pattern and rhythm the machine will perform and will allow for diversity in rhythm patterns and stroke length that aren't possible on the analog machine." Marlon makes a frozen fruit smoothie in a blender as we speak. He needs to attend a parent-teacher conference when we are done.

He ponders the end-user's expectations, continuing, "Do you want a rhythm you can predict and 'hang onto,' or something graduated and surprising? Or do you want something that builds like a piece of classical music might build? Hell, you could play a symphony and get hammered to that!"

But, unlike many sex machine inventors, Marlon claims he keeps his libido out of it. "I simply want to make something that speaks for itself, is marketable, and does the job in the most creative and satisfying way. You need to remember that, for this to make any sense in my life, it needs to be viable from a business perspective. I have a very tolerant girlfriend who has zero interest in any of this. She's never seen it, never wants to see it. For me to go forward with this, it needs to be a financial home run."

I sit on the floor, setting up the photograph. To my right is a balcony with a view onto the common area of the apartment complex, where people hurry from their cars with groceries and kids ride their bikes. The contrast between the surreal, larger-than-life sex machine sitting on the flowery couch, and the mundane everyday activities going on outside makes me want to laugh, as I'm feeling strangely embarrassed.

★ ★ ★

The sex machine underground doesn't look anything like I thought it would. Coming from sexually tolerant San Francisco, I was used to the idea that a sexual subculture would have its own style of dress, visual codes, and affectations, as does a lot of the BDSM community. Or perhaps I expected at least the stereotype of a sexual community as seen in our annual Folsom Street Fair, a leather-clad pageant that attracts thousands of visitors each year. But behind the sex machines stood everyday working guys—kind of like your high school shop teacher—who were married, had kids, liked to work in the shop and to make sex toys. It was all very suburban. No piercings, no tattoos, no leather. Nothing to group them together, and nothing to give away even a hint of a sexual subculture.

The sex machine, in every era and every part of the world, describes a modern icon: technology-meets-flesh. But all that these machines really do is one thing, the same thing, over and over: They thrust in and out of an orifice, in a wholly mechanical movement. The machines have become a form of contemporary folk art that reflects the ideas and quirks of their creators—yet in their essence, today's American sex machines can all be described simply as a large mechanical thrusting and turning device with a rubber penis attached. To someone who might see elegance in heavy industry, grace in machinery, and sensuality in mechanical movement, the American sex machine looks like a practical joke created in a high school shop class. Each machine appears to be some type of cartoonish male icon: mechanical, grandly phallic, perpetually hard, obviously devoid of emotion, and looking like its parts were all found at any local hardware store.

When plugged in and turned on, however, the machines deliver a strong, overwhelming presence in the room: Their sound fills the room with a mechanical, repetitive hum, and their movements look frightening. The machines' movements are so confident and determined in their attempts to re-create a human, sexual thrusting that in a way they are overdoing it, doing it stronger, faster, more precisely. And these attributes are the very things that make the machines seem like things I just don't want to touch. They seem dangerous. They seem like something so far away from qualities that are sensual or human.

Dick Check

Chris Ohnesorge

My coworker and I figured out that I'd seen about sixty-three cocks on my first night. This was certainly not something I could've boasted at any job I'd had before. But working at a gay sex club was not exactly your run-of-the-mill employment situation. I first decided to apply for the job of door person/bouncer at the club when Jason, a coworker from my dot-com day job, told me he worked there at the clothes check counter on weekends to make extra cash. He disclosed this when the two of us, along with three other fellow work fags, were having drinks and discussing our various states of dissatisfaction with our go-nowhere lives at a large online music and entertainment website. While I was making more money than I ever had before, I was still one of the lowest paid people there, and the droning repetition of my quality assurance position made all other employment sound lively and fascinating. And the chance to work at a job where I could see lots of naked gay men sounded like the perfect combination of extra cash and guaranteed sleaze to give my working life the kick in the ass it needed. Not to mention the fact that I had a major boner for Jason, and seeing him in the undies and boots attire that the clothes check guys usually wore was an added incentive.

The following Friday night I headed over to the club to "interview" with the manager, Gary. Everyone who worked there called it The Slut Hut. When I walked up to the main entrance, a door painted black to blend in with the exterior walls of the building, I realized I'd walked by this place hundreds of times without knowing it was a sex club. I was buzzed in and waited in the foyer, a nondescript 10 x 10 space with beige walls and a little booth where someone would sit and collect money, and sign people in.

My interview consisted of Gary, a handsome, dark-haired, mustached, Daddy-ish type in his midforties, asking me how I knew Jason. I told him about my regular job, and explained that I used to work at a porn shop that had preview booths and a triple-X theater, so a sexual environment wouldn't freak me out at all—even though I'd never set foot inside an *actual* sex club, which I never told him. He told me to start the next weekend and that I would work alternating weekends since the shifts were late (10 P.M. to 6 A.M.) and I had a regular job during the week. All I would have to do was sit by the door, buzz people in, and escort anyone out who was obviously high or became a nuisance. I was also to process new members, guests of members, and people coming to the club because they were on a list for a special party that night.

I discovered that "processing" was the main part of my duties. Processing consisted of me taking each man aside after he paid his fee or filled out a membership form and asking if he was a cop or worked for the NYPD, FBI, or any other law enforcement agency. Once he answered no to all these questions, I'd have him step behind a maroon velvet curtain and take his dick out for me. Now, I'm sure a lot of you are thinking, "Yeah, get *me* a job like that," but I was made to understand that "dick check" was strictly to cover the club's collective asses, so to speak. In New York City, if an on-duty law enforcement agent does not identify himself or herself when questioned or exposes himself or herself on duty, he or she is breaking the law. Even though the club was private, everything sexual happened in the back play space, which had to be entered through a door one was buzzed into, and no one underage was allowed in. This was Mayor Giuliani's New York City, and we were exactly the kind of place he loved to see shut down. But, legalities aside, the prospect of seeing a wide variety of dicks on the job was both amusing and titillating. Most places have a coat check attendant—here, I was the dick check attendant.

On my way to the club for my first Friday shift, all sorts of thoughts duked it out in my brain. Would I be horny the whole time, even though I wasn't working in the actual play area? Would guys at the club hit on me when I walked through the back to use the bathroom? Would the cops come in and bust the place and I'd go to jail? Would some hated ex come in as a member and have sex with all kinds of hot guys while I stewed and seethed on my little stool by the door? And just how many dicks would I get to see, anyway?

I think the thing that amazed me the most was how quickly the novelty of my job wore off. In the span of one eight-hour shift I went from being secretly giddy about all the penises I was going to see to being totally jaded about the whole experience. Although the occasional, raring-to-go patron was all boned-up and ready for action when I had him step behind the curtain, most of the guys I saw weren't hard, and to be honest, one can only get so excited by an unending succession of flaccid members.

As far as the possibility of sexual overtures from any of the club members on my way to use the bathroom facilities, I had far more pressing issues to concern myself with. Most importantly, I had to concentrate on remembering to touch as few of the surfaces within the club as was humanly possible every time I needed to use the bathroom. This was unfortunately often, given the number of bottles of energy-infused Vitamin Water I consumed and the tiny bladder I seem to possess. My boss used to joke that he was going to pay me extra to come in on the monthly watersports-themed nights because I'd be a hit with all the club-goers who wanted to get peed on.

There were three bathrooms in the club, two of which were located at the back end of the play space and one that was downstairs by a set of lockers and a shower room. I generally gravitated toward the downstairs bathroom in my first few shifts because I was intimidated by having to walk through all the sex, even though I was fully clothed. But while I avoided most of the sexual situations, there was one thing I had to beware of: the railing that ran down the set of stairs to the bathroom below. When walking down a flight of stairs, it's fairly instinctive for me to take hold of a railing if one is available. But every time I touched it, I was greeted by a very cold and slippery substance that was possibly lube, jizz, or a combination of the two. Each time I'd yank my hand back in disgust, but on the next trip down I'd forget and inevitably touch again what I began to call the Railing of Certain Grossness. I often worried that I'd have syphilis by the end of my shift.

But there were two beacons of hope on my first night at the club, and they came in the forms of Chance and Nate. Chance was an incredibly charismatic, twenty-two-year-old butchy/faggy dyke who worked at the money and sign-in window and acted as Gary's assistant manager. She had jet-black hair styled into a pompadour and wore fantastic vintage suits, and the best-smelling men's cologne I'd ever encountered. She'd always offset her masculine outfits with a pink neck scarf or outrageous false eyelashes and made me wish, on more than one occasion, that she actually were a boy because she'd have been such a perfect boyfriend for me. She was sarcastic and worldly, and we shared a mutual love/hate relationship with pop culture and celebrity. We became fast friends, hanging out on non–work nights bar hopping all over the East Village. She helped the time at work fly by, and I always dreaded my shifts without her and our nonstop conversations on everything from pop music to radical politics.

Nate, by contrast, was a lean, rockabilly-looking guy with sandy hair reminiscent of James Dean's, gorgeous tattoos, and gray-blue eyes that Chance and I officially deemed "dreamy." Even though I had a crush on the coworker who helped me get this job, he and I didn't work many shifts together, so Nate slid into the top spot as workplace object of lust. He'd often pop out, shirtless, from the clothes check counter to chat with me and Chance during slow times, and when he retreated back to his post we'd giggle and whisper like hyperactive schoolgirls.

As my dick check shifts at The Slut Hut accumulated, I got more and more used to my surroundings and started to enjoy the job. I loved working with Chance, especially when we got to work on our favorite monthly theme night, "Spank Me Hard," also known as "Popcorn Night." The first time I arrived for Popcorn Night, which is how Chance referred to it, I checked my schedule and all I saw listed was "Spank Me Hard." When I asked what Popcorn Night was, she refused to tell me and simply smiled knowingly and murmured, "Oh, just you wait." As visions of kinky goings-on involving popcorn shoved into buttered orifices flashed horrifically through my mind—hello, salty things don't go there!—patrons began arriving. After about fifteen minutes I heard this muted, slapping sound coming from the back room at random intervals. Chance watched me with a bemused grin as my eyes widened and met hers in recognition of the sound. We both burst into simultaneous, tear-inducing laughter—she at my sudden realization, and me at the absurdly unsexy noise of what sounded like some huge bag of popcorn popping in a microwave. From then on, Popcorn Night became my favorite night to work and I always bought a bag of prepackaged popcorn on my way to work to commemorate the event.

After my first few weekends I decided to use the more conveniently located bathrooms at the back of the club. Aside from being able to avoid the slimy railing, I would be able to indulge my voyeuristic fantasies on my trips to and from the toilet. Because I had clothes on, most patrons recognized me as an employee and ignored me. But some of them, because of either genuine attraction or substance-induced lust, saw me as a novel person to hit on: somebody with actual clothes to take off! One night, while leaving the bathroom, a glassy-eyed, pint-sized, totally naked Latino guy bumped into me on my way back out to the dick check station. He wobbled before me, staring at me as if sizing up a painting in a museum, and then unceremoniously turned around, bent over, and spread his asscheeks with both hands, awaiting my enjoyment. I stifled a bubbling giggle that felt more than a little hysterical, slapped him on the ass, and shouted, "Thanks anyway, sport!" and raced to tell Chance all about my encounter.

On a particularly crazed Saturday night when it seemed like every gay man in New York was packed into our medium-sized back room, a ridiculously gorgeous guy came in to sign up for a membership. He looked like he could've been Lenny Kravitz's stunt double, in his burnt-umber leather coat, tight flared jeans, and black lace-front shirt. He had a close-cropped Afro and a permanently mischievous grin he kept flashing in my direction. When he came over to me for the usual Q and A followed by dick check, he maintained eye contact with me the whole time, never losing that smirk. When I took him behind the curtain, he seemed to take extra time pulling out his cock, watching me the whole time to see if I was savoring the experience. I was. He was one of the few—and I mean few—men who came in that had a really appealing flaccid cock. It looked heavy, warm, and soft to touch. I really had to stop myself from finding out if it was. He asked me if I liked what I saw and I managed the least casual "Yeah" I've ever uttered. When he inquired if he'd see me in the back, I sputtered something about not playing on the job. I was completely flummoxed; men like him absolutely, positively never hit on me and, while it flattered me to no end, next to him I felt as sexy as a shrub.

As the night progressed, I fought the urge to pee, despite the huge bottle of water I'd consumed in my first hour of work. Finally, when I felt like my bladder was going to literally explode out of my body, I ventured to the back. I decided that if Mr. Unbelievably Hot approached me maybe I'd at least make out with him a little bit and try to get in a grope or two. Even something that first-base with such a gorgeous guy would be enough of an ego-boost for the next decade. Despite the fact that the clothes check guys played in the sex rooms during their shifts all the time, and my boss, Gary, practically lived back there fucking numerous guys every night the club was open, I wasn't supposed to stray from the dick check station except to use the restroom or run across the street for snacks. As I made my way to the back, I tried to seem really nonchalant as I scanned the dark room for him. I caught a glimpse of him out of the corner of my eye, fucking a muscular, shaved-headed white guy against a wooden platform. He flashed me that killer smile and

I stood rooted in place, watching his tightly muscled, sweat-slick body in motion. After a moment or two, I noticed something that broke my reverie: He wasn't wearing a condom.

I think my jaw might have actually dropped like some surprised cartoon character. In my mind, every man at the club must be practicing safe sex, especially with so many strangers involved. I retreated to the bathroom, emptied my bladder, and collected myself. Maybe he knew the guy. Maybe he was his boyfriend and they just liked to do it in public. Walking back toward the dick check area, I watched a lot of the other patrons more keenly. I saw two guys fucking against a wall, also condom-less. A line of eight men stood waiting to fuck a guy in a sling, and not one of them even had a condom in his hand.

Back at my stool by the front door, I mulled over what I'd seen in the last few minutes. I thought it took a lot to shock me sexually. Even if I hadn't done everything there was to do in the wide world of fucking, I was certainly aware of it. After a few friendships with pro-dommes, former hustlers, and a variety of friends who stripped their way through college, nothing fazed me much. But I suddenly felt like a seven-year-old kid seeing his teacher outside of school for the first time. I told Chance and Nate, who had joined us out front for a snack break, about what I'd seen and they seemed to chuckle in unison. They told me that safe sex was pretty much the exception to the rule at the club and even though there were condoms on shelves all over the play area, usage of them wasn't enforced at all. I chewed this information over and over for the rest of the night. In some ways, it all seemed really stupid and dangerous. But at the same time, these were grown men who could make their own choices, and knew the risks they were taking, so who was I to judge? By the end of my shift, it started to become yet another thing I felt jaded about—an increasingly familiar state of being for me at The Slut Hut.

A few weeks previous, I'd mustered up the nerve to ask Nate out on a date. I did it with my usual sarcastic, self-deprecating brand of charm, figuring I could pass it all off as a joke if he wasn't into the idea. He started to protest on the grounds of not dating co-workers, and I countered by saying, "It's not dating, it's a *date,*" a brilliant reply if ever I'd had one. He agreed and I told Chance as soon as I could get her alone. She was excited and totally jealous, and we immediately began discussing date outfits. But our planning was abruptly halted when we ran into him the night before the intended date during one of our work-free, bar-hopping evenings. I attempted breezy conversation with Nate while Chance waited in line for cocktails. In the middle of my blathering on about how much I hated my nine-to-five job he said, "Can we just be friends?"

"Sure, yeah. I mean, sure. What?" I replied with stunning articulation. He answered me with the time-honored phrase that has been used since man first crawled up out of the primordial ooze and started breaking hearts:

"I like you, I'm just not *into* you that way."

This time I got what he was saying loud and clear. For fear of seeming overly dramatic, I sat and nursed the gin and tonic Chance bought me for all of five minutes before I excused myself with a headache or malaria or some equally believable excuse, hopped in a cab, and headed back to my regular, no-date-on-the-horizon existence. Conveniently, Nate seemed to grow exponentially less attractive with each encounter I had with him at work. When I told Chance about what he'd said, she was pissed beyond belief and swore he must have the worst taste in men ever. See why I adored her?

My hurt lasted for all of two weeks till Nate was all but forgotten during a rare shift I worked with Jason on the Sunday night of a three-day weekend. I ran into Jason on my way out of one of the back bathrooms for the fifth time that night. He was wearing a leather vest, boots, and a well-worn jockstrap. I tried to look at his face as we chatted, instead of eyeing him as lasciviously as I wanted to. After a minute I noticed he was talking to me but his attention was focused across the room on two men rutting like bulls on a raised wooden platform. I glanced down and watched as his right hand slid languidly along his thick, long erection. I think I actually gulped. He had alluded to being big, in a joking way, but it was no joke. Before he even saw me gaping, I dashed back to dick check, afraid that this might overstep some sort of coworker/friend boundary. A year later, after a handful of drunken, secretive encounters, I'd laugh about how silly I acted over seeing Jason's dick. But after that night he replaced Nate and, once again, became my number one work infatuation.

I'm sure that working at a sex club isn't necessarily something that one considers a source of long-term employment, but for me it lasted a miniscule four months. It wasn't anything to do with Nate that made me leave, or the Railing of Certain Grossness. It wasn't the late hours, the occasional patron in a K-hole that I had to dress and escort from the club, or even some moral indignation at the truckloads of unsafe sex that went on. It was my boss. But it wasn't the fact that, despite his good nature and inclination to pay me really well for a job that required very little brainpower, he was a micromanaging control freak who did too much crystal meth on the job and was also a sex addict who seemed to have opened the club so he could fuck as many men as he could get his hands on. Nope, not even all that. It was the fact that I suddenly realized he reminded me of my dad.

A week before my final shift at the Hut, my mom sent me a

package with a bunch of color copies of old photos she'd been organizing and putting into new albums. A number of them were from the early 1970s, right after I'd been born, when she and my dad were still married. In them my father sported the slightly shaggy hair and squared-off, porn star mustache that was de rigueur for that time. I enjoyed the pictures and cracked up over my parents' polyester outfits and then put them away. But at work that Saturday I was stopped by Gary on my way back from restocking the paper towels in the downstairs bathroom. He told me the free-soda fridge by the clothes check area was running low and that there were more boxes of pop in his office. He told me all of this while naked and stroking his lube-covered erection. At that moment, a barrage of images of my dad in those old photos—along with the childhood memory of seeing him naked when I burst in on him and his girlfriend after a nightmare—filled my head and I realized in utter horror that Gary looked exactly like my father. At the end of my shift I took him aside and told him I didn't think I could handle the hours anymore and that it was impacting my day job. He was a little disappointed but he said he understood, gave me a goodbye kiss on the cheek (still naked!), and wished me well.

I stayed friends with Chance and delighted in her stories of Nate's declining performance at work and how she took him out for drinks one night to gently fire him. As soon as she began mentioning his absenteeism and how he spent more time blowing guys than working the clothes check counter, he must've realized why he was there because he stood up and ran out of the bar, never to return to The Slut Hut again. I've still never gone to a sex club as a patron, and I probably never will. My mother once spent the summer working at a donut shop, and to this day she wouldn't eat a single donut if you paid her. After my four months as dick checker at The Slut Hut, I think the last thing I could do in a sex

The following text was inadvertently left off page 120:

"club would be to actually have sex. If anything, I'd probably just want to go clean off the railing."

The publisher regrets the error.

Best Sex Writing 2005
Edited by Violet Blue
Cleis Press
ISBN 1-57344-217-8

Sex with the Imperfect Stranger
Patrick Califia

November 20 is a day of remembrance for the transgendered community to honor our beloved dead. In 2001, transactivists said that
one person was reported killed every month because of prejudice
against transgendered people. This phraseology is used because not
all the victims of prejudice against transgenderism are themselves
cross-dressers or transsexual. They include, for example, people like
Calpernia Addams's boyfriend, Barry Winchell. He was a soldier
who was killed by two other men in his unit who felt incensed that
his lover was a transgendered woman. The death of Gwen Araujo
(born Eddie) makes November 20 an especially somber day.

As I write this I am looking at an undated photograph of Gwen
(who sometimes called herself Lida). She is wearing a hooded
sweatshirt, holding a baby, and smiling, looking like any high
school girl babysitting for one of her mother's friends. It is painful
and disturbing to imagine her dead body, wrapped in a blanket,

buried in a shallow grave in a remote campground. When one of the people who had witnessed her murder led police to that hiding place, she still had a rope wrapped around her neck. She had been stabbed several times and beaten. When I read the account of her injuries, I feel as if I too am a witness of the fury and, yes, terror that reportedly drove a group of young men to murder her. It is as if she had to be killed over and over again. This is a common (if such savagery can be described by that banal word) characteristic of the murders of transgender women.

Michael Magidson, twenty-seven; Jason Nabors, nineteen; Paul Merel, Jr., twenty-five; and Paul's brother, José Merel, twenty-four, were arrested on suspicion of homicide. Magidson, Nabors, and José Merel were charged with murder and the commission of a hate crime. (California is one of only five states that include gender identity in their hate crime laws.) A fourth suspect, Jason Cazares, twenty-two, was recently charged solely with murder.

On October 3, the day that she died, Gwen was seventeen. According to news accounts, she went to a party that was fated to turn ugly. Although Gwen had worn women's clothes for several years, she had never worn a skirt in public before. She was apparently nervous about this, because she took a pair of pants with her to change into if the more feminine outfit became uncomfortable or dangerous. At the party, she reportedly had a few beers and had anal sex with José Merel, a boy she had a crush on, and perhaps with a friend of his, Michael Magidson. Things started to go wrong when Nicole Brown, the girlfriend of José's brother, followed Gwen into the bathroom (or, by some accounts, took her in there) and discovered that she wasn't a biological female. "It's a man, let's go," she called out, and the attack began.

This makes it sound like the people at the party had no idea that Gwen Araujo was not born male. But according to one of Araujo's friends, Stephanie Baumann, she didn't pass. "I don't understand how those men could say they had no idea he was a guy. If you just saw him, you'd know," she told reporters from the *San Jose Mercury News*. Several other details reported in this case do not ring true. It is reported that Araujo had an altercation with the suspects about a week before the party. (She had also been found unconscious in front of a church near her home a few weeks before the murder. Her mother said she had been beaten.)

This was someone who had been insisting on wearing makeup and women's clothing and using a female name since she was fourteen. She had frequently been taunted and threatened. She'd been unable to find a job locally because of her gender expression. Why would she willingly attend a social event with people who hated her—unless she was lured to that party? Or, as one source suggests, she was dating one of the men who are now charged with killing her. The "gender check" apparently performed by one of the arrested men's girlfriend is also suspicious. It is quite reasonable to ask if the sex that reportedly took place was consensual. Paul Merel says his girlfriend woke him up and made him leave the party with her when the attack began, but he also says he saw Araujo on the floor with her skirt pulled up. That sort of exposure smacks of sexual humiliation if not outright rape. It's also possible that if one of the men present was her boyfriend, he was utterly and completely humiliated when Gwen's biological sex was publicly exposed, and was so afraid for his own reputation that he became enraged and violent.

In a small town like Newark, California, it is doubtful that everyone at the party was completely ignorant of Gwen's gender status. Gossip like that travels far and fast. And the defendants were well-enough known to her for their names to appear in a Harry Potter address book that police found in her belongings. "We're dealing with a number of people [at the party] who could have helped, stepped in, prevented or reported this," says Newark Police Lt. Lance Morrison. "None of them did."

Gwen's mother reported her missing when she did not come home from the party. Scary rumors about her fate circulated for two weeks until one of the partygoers cracked. Jason Nabors contacted the police and took them to where Gwen's body was buried, 150 miles into the Sierra Nevada foothills. The location was so remote that it could only be reached by a four-wheel-drive vehicle. Morrison described the crime scene as "haunting and gruesome."

I'm not sure why this murder of a transgendered person has gotten so much more attention in the press than previous cases, like the June 2001 murder of two-spirited Fredericka Martinez, a sixteen-year-old Navajo from Cortez, Colorado. Bay Area cultural critic David Steinberg speculates it's because the death took place in Newark, California, near the "proudly open-minded, relatively diversity-accepting San Francisco Bay Area," and because Gwen had strong support and acceptance from her family. Her youth and beauty make her a sympathetic figure. She had been driven out of public school by her bigoted peers, she had problems with drugs and alcohol. Maybe the poignant deaths of Brandon Teena and Matthew Shepherd have tenderized the conscience of the mass media. The high school that could not tolerate Araujo's attendance was, ironically enough, producing *The Laramie Project,* a play about the Wyoming murder of Shepherd, a gay man who was pistol whipped, tied to a fence, and left to freeze to death by two men who later claimed he had propositioned them.

Stories about Gwen's death appeared on CNN, in *USA Today,* and in the *New York Times.* Although generally sympathetic in tone, articles about the case often referred to her as a cross-dresser and used male pronouns. (Araujo's mother suffered from the same problem, referring to her transgendered child as "he" even while revealing her plans to bury Gwen in female clothing and put the name Gwen on her headstone.) But a spate of letters from readers who felt this was an insult to the dead girl moved the *San Francisco Chronicle* to editorialize about the "pronoun problem," and an article it ran about Jack Thompson, a female-to-male, teenaged transman, was carefully edited to refer to him as such. Reporter Kelly St. John insisted on this usage, and the newspaper is considering the updated Associated Press style, which calls for use of the pronoun consistent with the way a transgendered individual lives publicly. (Old guidelines had insisted on using the birth name and sex assigned at birth until after sex-change surgery.)

Sadly, the killing of Araujo did not end her persecution. She was buried on October 25 in a casket adorned with butterflies. Her mother had dressed her in a lace blouse and had her fingernails done in rainbow glitter. The Rev. Jeff Finley eulogized Gwen, saying, "I wonder how many times Eddie cried in secret, wondering, where do I fit in? Maybe we were not there enough for you, because we did not understand." But Araujo's family was probably remembering the night before, when the notorious publicity hound and homo-hate-monger Fred Phelps dared to show up with a band of twenty-three of his crazed followers and picketed her mother's house, bearing signs that read, EDDIE's IN HELL.

Araujo's case has been prominently featured on Phelps's website, www.godhatesfags.com, as well as the website of the Army of God and other right-wing Christian organizations. Right-wingers were also quick to take umbrage at the compassionate and respectful tone taken by more liberal newspapers. One critic ridiculed "the liberal Hate Crimes crowd" and "the ridiculous whining that began right after Araujo's death, about the media not using the 'correct' pronouns or names in their coverage of the story.... Never mind that journalists are required to report the facts of a given news story...such points as a subject's gender and legal name." I've yet to see an article about the case that did not include Araujo's birth name and the sex she was assigned at birth. But even such a trifling matter as including the name that she preferred to be called is seen by conservatives as a very big step down the slippery slope toward (gasp) social acceptance of transgendered people. "[P]art of the campaign to further 'understanding of transgender issues' is to indoctrinate, or to use a more politically correct term, to *educate* children on such subjects in school," sniped the right-wing Chron Watch website. The person responsible for this editorial seems oblivious to the fact that Gwen Araujo was a child who went to school, a school where she found no safety. And school systems that keep silent about homosexuality and transgenderism teach queer bashers—indeed, taught the murderers of Gwen Araujo—that it was socially acceptable to target butch girls and femme boys.

The most twisted response to this 5'6", slightly built teenager's death has to be an article by Zach Calef that appeared in the *Iowa State Daily*. Let's not forget that Araujo not only suffered blunt force trauma to the head, she was also tied up, stabbed in the face and body, and dragged into the garage where a rope was tied around her neck by a crowd of assailants, who then strangled her. But Calef terms this violence as "simply a reaction to a form of rape." Throughout this screed, Calef refers to Araujo as "he" and says, "He tricked them into having sex with him, but if they would have known his sex, they wouldn't have been interested. That is just as bad as rape." He concedes, "Given the circumstances, murder is a bit much," but suggests Magidson et al. were "not in a normal mind set when they acted...probably 'temporarily insane'" and so should be "charged with manslaughter or something along those lines." Calef even has the gall to argue that the murder is not a hate crime, because according to him, that would mean "the underlying reason for the beating was Araujo's sexual orientation. And that is not the case. The men did what they did because Araujo violated them. He used lies and deception to trick them into having sex. He was not honest with them and had he been, none of this would have happened. A hate crime should not even be considered. No one killed him because he was a cross-dresser. These men were truly violated. They were raped."

It's fascinating that Calef assumes that he knows so much about what happened between this transgendered teenager and the men who reportedly fucked and then murdered her. His scenario is based on a dreary stereotype that is horribly familiar to anyone who has followed legal cases in which ostensibly straight men are charged with assaulting or killing gay men or transgendered people. These defendants always argue that it was the queer who came on to them, who used deceit or force in an attempt to wring some sexual gratification out of them. Defense attorneys try (with a depressing amount of success) to get judges and juries to see their clients' violent behavior much as Calef does—as a perfectly understandable state of rage that springs from a feeling of having been violated. This strategy relies on widespread social acceptance of the belief that this is what straight men are supposed to do when their heterosexual identities are threatened. They are supposed to murder in defense of their masculinity. Because if one of them doesn't do this, if he does not violently repudiate the possibility that he found it pleasurable to have sexual contact with someone who was not born female, then he must be queer himself. (What often goes unstated is the corollary that this would then make him liable to stigma and assault.)

Sex with a new person is always a risk, whether you're on a

blind date or hiring a sex worker. You are always going to come out of such an encounter with information about the other person that you didn't have before. (And they are going to carry away some secrets about you, as well.) I am always skeptical about the claims made by johns who say they had no idea the gorgeous girl they screwed was "really a guy" [*sic*]. But even if his astonishment is real, what is the appropriate response? If I find out that somebody I had sex with is really married, and this is a huge disappointment to me, or morally offensive, does that justify killing them? Of course not. Suppose I've tried something new, something I never thought I would like, and after the pleasure is over, I feel upset about what I've done. Remorse is often the precursor to self-knowledge. So I have a lot to think about. I may decide I never want to do that again, and I may work through my shame or anxiety and integrate this new pleasure into my repertoire. What I absolutely ought not to do is attempt to obliterate the person who set this uncomfortable but pretty common process in motion. If you don't get what you want out of a sexual encounter, you may have very powerful feelings about it, but the right thing to do is put your pants or panties back on, and take your feelings with you when you leave.

The number of gay men or transgendered people who feel powerful enough to try to pressure a straight guy into having sex with them—let alone actually rape him—is miniscule. The victim in such cases is usually deliberately sought out by the attackers; hunted down; and intimidated, battered, or slaughtered. Violence against sexual minority people is a sport. And the number of straight men who occasionally or habitually have sex with other men or with male-to-female transgendered people is so high that the word "heterosexual" ought to always have quotes around it. Given the fact that the men accused of killing Araujo are known to have harassed her before they took her life, it seems highly unlikely that they were shocked by her genitalia. Perhaps what really happened is that they were caught enjoying sex with someone who was not a socially sanctioned object of desire. They were, it's reasonable to suspect, quite happy to make use of her body as long as that activity wasn't a matter of public knowledge. This would make them hypocrites, not rape victims.

The creepy illogic that informs Calef's infamous article is so pervasive that the right wing is using the defamatory stereotype of transgendered people as sexual predators to attack civil rights legislation. The National Transgender Advocacy Coalition (NTAC) has protested attack ads circulated shortly before voters were asked to retain or repeal an equal rights ordinance in Ypsilanti, Michigan. This bedroom community of fewer than 23,000 people has been under a relentless right-wing siege to overturn its civil rights ordinance ever since it was passed in 1997. All previous attempts have failed. Among the ordinance's opponents are Tom Monaghan, an antiabortion activist and the wealthy ex-CEO of Domino's Pizza; former Green Bay Packer Reggie White; a religious soul group called the Winans Sisters; and Ypsilanti Citizens Voting Yes for Equal Rights not Special Rights. The Ypsilanti Campaign for Equality, which does not have the big budget of the forces for repeal, has gone door-to-door to counter ads that feature a picture of a preoperative transsexual with the caption, "Will you vote YES to protect your daughter...your granddaughter...from being forced to use the girl's bathroom with men like this?"

NTAC chair Vanessa Edwards Foster responds, "It's misleading, and very provocative. They implant the message of 'protect your daughters' with the false image that male-to-female transgenders all somehow rape or molest. It's only a step away from the Klan movie *Birth of a Nation* implying a need to protect your daughters by saying that all black men wanted to rape white women. These broad generalizations are not only inaccurate, they're defamatory and damaging to an entire class of people."

Speaking as a preoperative transgender person who is sometimes forced to use public restrooms, I want to point out that we are the people who are especially at risk there. Even when I go into a stall and lock the door, I am always afraid to take my pants down while other men make use of nearby urinals and stalls. It has been more than a year since anybody challenged my gender identity in public. But if the difference between my face and my genitals is ever going to become an explosive issue, it is there, and I hate it. Gwen Araujo was someone's daughter. She was someone's granddaughter. And her biological sex was exposed in a place that was supposed to be private, by an intrusive straight woman, who may have then incited the men at the party to kill her. Nontransgendered people don't need protection from us in public bathrooms or elsewhere. *We* need protection from *them*.

Among the people whom Araujo needed protection from was her own therapist. Between the ages of fourteen and sixteen, she is reported to have worked with Linda Skerbec. Skerbec is associated with the Focus on the Family ministry, that bizarre organization in Colorado that sponsors "National Coming Out of Homosexuality Day." Focus on the Family endorses so-called "reparative therapy" to change gay people into heterosexuals, a dubious and ineffective practice that has been condemned by the American Psychological Association. After Araujo's death, Skerbec told one reporter that she was about to persuade her client to "move beyond the label" of transgender and "claim the sexual identity that matched his anatomy. To me, Eddie was very much a male, a creative, sensitive male. But I worried some. I knew that kids like Eddie could be hurt." Why, yes—by mental health professionals who are unethical, poorly trained, and blinded by hateful religious ideology. With "support" like this, no wonder Araujo had problems with drugs and alcohol, couldn't pursue her education, and engaged in other self-destructive behavior.

Like any adolescent, Gwen Araujo was coming into her sexuality. The need to explore this aspect of her being was legitimate and developmentally appropriate. How sad and terrible it is that the desire she felt to be pretty, to attract a man's attention, to feel wanted and loved and admired, came upon her in a setting where she was perceived as less than human. She got the death penalty for wanting to party like any suburban teenager who is nearly out of high school, nearly an adult. And she joined the ranks of many other transgendered people who were seen as so inhuman that they had to be obliterated.

Disrespect and hatred for transgendered bodies is common even when we cannot be hurt or killed. Tyra Hunter was a male-to-female, preoperative transsexual woman who was unlucky enough to be in a life-threatening car accident. The paramedics who arrived at the scene cut off her pants to tend her wounds, discovered genitals that appeared to be male, and delayed treating her while they insulted her. They were so afraid or unwilling to touch her body that they may have contributed to her death. Hunter's family took the rare action of pursuing legal action against these men, who were firefighters from Engine Company 30. The same engine company was called to the scene when two transgendered women in the Washington, D.C., area were gunned down in their car on August 12 of this year. One of the so-called "Dirty Thirty" dragged Stephanie Thomas, aged nineteen, out of her car and dropped the body face-first onto the ground. Later on, a firefighter pushed her body over with his foot as blood poured from her head and neck wounds. An eyewitness says the firefighters were apparently afraid to touch Thomas or the other victim, Ukea Davis, eighteen.

Why is it a capital crime, a cause for vigilante action, for a woman to have a penis, or for a man to have a vagina? The body is inherently both marvelous and flawed. When we reach out to another person, we bring our flaws with us, along with the potential for escaping into the magic of sensuality. No one is as much of a man or a woman as they'd like to be; no one exposes their body without thinking, if only briefly, about what is wrong with it. Yet most of us manage to find our way to pleasure, in part because sexual ecstasy obliterates our awareness of or our anxiety about all our shortcomings.

In clinical terms, I am a preoperative female-to-male transsexual. This presupposes, of course, that until I let a surgeon alter my genitals, I am incomplete. However, receiving that surgery is no guarantee that anyone will see me as male. No matter how I look, my female history will remain a defining characteristic. I will always have to struggle to maintain some kind of positive relationship to that history. It is like being my own mother—the long years I spent in the lesbian community gradually giving birth to this bearded face, this flat chest, this hairy belly, this transman. I feel a perpetual tension between my desire to leave the past behind, to live completely as male, and the feeling that I owe a certain amount of respect to my progenitor, and have a duty to acknowledge her in a loving way.

Like Gwen Araujo and any transsexual, pre-, post-, or nonoperative, I confront the dilemma of how to express my identity, seek out love, and express my sexuality. The ambiguity of my own body is supposed to prevent me from doing this. I am supposed to dislike my body so much that I can't touch myself, let alone allow another person to touch me. *No*, I say to that proscription. Being gender dysphoric is hard enough without being denied all human touch, even my own.

Preop tranny girls complain about the men who have sex with them who are closeted gays or bisexuals. Most of them don't want a male lover who is drawn to them because they still have their penises. But you can touch a penis in such a way that your hand conveys your understanding that it represents a clitoris. Between her balls, there is an invisible vulval cleft that yearns for recognition and occupation. It can flare into reality with the right verbal encouragement, a lubricated finger drawn down the crease. The ass can be a pussy. A trannyboy's cunt can become his ass, or his lover can caress him in such a way that it isn't there at all, and only one hole exists, the one that "should" be there. An FTM's clitoris can become the cock that it would have changed into if fetal androgens had circulated in his mother's womb. All of these are stopgap measures, fantasies, shared beliefs, a tantric magic spell that may evaporate outside the bedroom. But sex is always magic, idealizing the other and oneself. Few of us leave the site of a potent tryst without losing the fairy dust that made us so perceptive, inventive, and fulfilled.

Can a person who is not transsexual understand how to make love that way? Yes, of course, sometimes. The closest I've come in the past is with leathermen who don't hesitate to say "Sir" when they ask to wear my collar or receive a lashing or a fat greasy dick. I'd read about femmes who learned how to pleasure their stone butch lovers. Testosterone opened a new erotic realm to me, the possibility that I might actually seek to bed the pretty women I admired, wrap their long legs around my waist. My most recent girl-friend is a femme who knows how to fuck, a femme who has had extremely masculine female lovers. But she doesn't like men. She's a dyke. In her work as a professional dominatrix she has a very firm boundary that forbids sexual contact with the men who pay her for humiliation, bondage, dominance, and pain. And so when I go to bed with her there is a world of misunderstanding between us, too many silences and too much fear in my heart.

Despite the fact that she occasionally dresses up in jeans and a flannel shirt, puts her dick on, and goes out drinking with her gay men friends, I don't think she has a clue about what it feels like to be transgendered, to have an inner sense of being someone other than the person that everyone else assumes you are. Yet she is very generous and careful with me. She allows me to touch her in any way that takes my fancy. She lets me say anything that I want to say. And she goes with me, her excitement follows my lead. I get this much latitude and trust because she likes the way my imagination works. We have the same fantasies, the same need to mingle tender caresses with well-targeted slaps, to heighten our excitement with physical restraint and role-playing. In bed, she is my ingénue and my tigress-whore, the blonde slut with perfect big breasts and the tightest box in the world. I want her constantly, especially when she says something cross and clever, or struggles against me while challenging me to do my best and my worst. I love touching her.

Usually I can't let her touch me. She is prone to making terrible mistakes about my gender, frequently calling me "she" in public. Most people fortunately don't hear the error, but when they do, it is embarrassing for me, and scary. She's surprised when I refuse to attend women-only events. When this happens I can't take my clothes off with her, can't let her touch me, in fact don't want to be with her at all. And I know then that there is a problem that cannot be solved between us, something that will ultimately separate us. I want to be a man more than she wants me to be one. While often feeling myself to be less than a man, to her I am too much of one, though she will never say so out loud.

She wants to fuck me, always, and cries sometimes when I tell her no. I wonder why I refuse her when I would almost certainly let a lover of mine who was an FTM penetrate me, or a bioguy. I like the way that it feels. I often have trouble coming with a partner, but vaginal penetration intensifies my orgasms with someone else. Is this my bullshit sexism, buying into some 1950s idea that men don't let their girlfriends fuck them? How can this be when I know so many men, bisexual or even straight, who want a finger or a dildo up the butt? The gay men I know feel that the more they get fucked, the more butch it makes them. I hate anal penetration, but if I feel fine about all these other men who bend over, why do I quibble about using a hole that I *do* like? Why hold myself back? Of course it's partly because I'm afraid that if she fucks me, she'll think I'm a girl. (Where have we heard *that* before?)

But one of the blessings of testosterone is the high-octane sex drive it produces that tends to eliminate such tender considerations. The last time we had sex, it was so good that when I finished having her, I didn't care what anybody else, including her, thought of me or my gender. I was weary of being a philanthropist in the bedroom, devoid of any capacity to enjoy one more iota of vicarious pleasure. I just wanted to come, more than once, and come hard. So I asked her to blow me, and she gave me some of the longest, sweetest, most tender head I've ever had. For once I had little or no anxiety about how she felt about moving her head up and down over my crotch instead of burrowing into it like a proper muff diver. "Fuck me, honey," I said after the third time I came, and she obliged me.

And when I came with her mouth around my cock and her fingers inside me, I had the strangest experience. I felt blessed by the specific quality of the good feelings that flooded my body and soul. Those contractions, in that wet place…how strong they were, how oddly masculine. It was an ejaculation without semen, but it was an inner pumping of bone-melting ecstasy, directed at the core of my soul. The target was not someone else's orifice, but my own. And I knew that this was pleasure I could not feel if I only had a cock, or for that matter if I had female genitals and had never taken testosterone. It was a transgendered orgasm, and as it brought tears to my eyes, I felt grateful to have a cunt. I didn't want to trade it for anybody else's genitals. And it was my partner's acceptance, the zone of care and safety she had created, that allowed me to have this release. That most imperfect of all strangers, me myself, had been welcome in a good home for just a little while.

But I think we must have that in common, you and I, trans or not. The last time you had really good sex with somebody you loved, someone who loved you—isn't that why it felt so good? Were you not looking for a sense that your partner was comfortable with and appreciative of your body, that he or she wanted you passionately and yet had respect for your limitations? Were you, too, knocked out by the sheer goodness of those despised parts of ourselves, the hidden sensitive skin that exists only to make us happy?

This is what I love about human nature: the fact that we can, each of us, be so different from one another, and yet so utterly the same. If we look at one another with love or at least respect instead of loathing, it is so easy to see what connects us. If only the men who had sex with Gwen Araujo had valued her, both as a woman and as a woman who had a penis, who was like any other girl they could have made love with, but who was also unique. Yes, we need more tolerance for our differences, our diversity, but we also need to be able to accept what we have in common. Because it was when someone could not stomach his response to Gwen Araujo, his ability to be close to her, to join with her, or to simply want her, that he became capable of wiping out her existence.

Gwen Araujo's murderers feared becoming like her, a faggot, a queer, a cross-dresser, a he-she, a transsexual freak. The larger culture did not value their unique capacity to lust after her, to find her beautiful. And there is indeed something queer about being attracted to transgendered people. Someone who is born male who chooses to give up the privileges associated with that state (or fails to win access to them) is a scary phenomenon. Because if even one person can shed their skin, defy the dictate of their genetic sex, and decide to be somebody else, well, couldn't we all make that choice? The fact that this decision is so resented would indicate that perhaps the manliest man and the womanliest woman are not very happy performing in those roles. It's uncomfortable to step back and look at the way that you behave, how you dress and talk, how you move through the world, what you want for yourself, how you judge your own worth as a person. Gender conditioning may be unpleasant for everybody, not just transsexuals. People who have willed themselves to perform a difficult task are often very angry at the people who do not feel the same sense of duty.

This is the kind of violence that legal reform cannot address. Transsexuals are hated because our existence breaks up the hegemony of "normal" social sex-roles and compulsory heterosexuality. In this era, the existence of "opposite sexes," male and female, is thought to be dictated by biology. This view of nature ignores a plethora of gender-fucking and same-sex activity among mammals, birds, fishes, reptiles, and insects. Gwen Araujo had to teach herself how to put on makeup. When she put on a skirt, she was perceived as pretending to be a woman, being a cross-dresser, going in drag. But her sisters and her mother had also been taught how to "put on" the clothing and mannerisms of women. If being a human female was a simple matter of obeying the dictates of biology, how much of this conditioning would be necessary? Why would it be necessary for our society to enforce such horrendous penalties upon people who violate these norms? Of course our physicality, our genetic inheritance, plays a huge role in our personalities and the presentation of self. But transsexuals are as much a part of nature as female babies born with vulvas and wombs who grow up to be feminine straight women. We belong here, too.

Khajuraho
Arlo Tolesco

The temples at Khajuraho were built between A.D. 950 and 1050. At some point—no one knows exactly when or why—the temples were abandoned and the entire area became enveloped by impenetrable jungle. When Mughal invaders galloped down from Central Asia and across the subcontinent, countless masterpieces of Hindu art and architecture were demolished. But in Khajuraho the temples hid, their pent-up sexual energy tucked away, awaiting a time when they would once again be known to the world.

In 1838, a group of British army men were hacking through the jungle with machetes when they happened upon the temples. Now, over a century and a half later, what exactly went on there still tantalizes us.

These days, most of the trees are gone, so no need to sharpen up the ol' machete. But nevertheless, Khajuraho, India, is a still a pain in the ass to get to—which is exactly why we ended up going there. We needed to go somewhere, anywhere, to escape the crush of *30 million* people heading home from the Kumbha Mela festival, the largest gathering of people ever in one day in the history of the earth.

With the main festivities over, a good portion of said 30 million were taking off for home or other nearby spiritual hot spots. With the entire transportation system bursting beyond capacity, getting anywhere was going to be a nightmare. And I don't mean the Oakland–San Francisco Bay Bridge at 6 P.M. on a Friday night. This was much, much worse.

Luckily, we'd joined up along the way with some older, wiser, more experienced American folk—spiritually awakened/ postneurotic/sacred loving types from Seattle (one of whom claimed to have invented smoothies). They told us there was a city they knew, not so far away. We just had to mash ourselves into one train and then another, and then a five-hour Jeep ride over treacherous, broken terrain.

Some fifty-two hours later, battered and road-weary, we're unpacking our bags and getting ready to collapse in our Khajuraho rooming house. We'd slept on train station floors and been crushed into trains for the last two days to get to this place I'd never heard of and knew nothing about and, most frustratingly, whose name I could not pronounce: *Kah-jer-RAH-hoe.*

A mercifully quiet, empty, little town.

So, that's how we got there, Anna and I. Arrived in Khajuraho in once piece, stone-tired but happy, with some idea that there were these "erotic temples" we were going to see in the morning.

The older folks split off and hunkered down in their own rooms to rest their aching backs and butts.

Now, for the first time in a long time, I'm alone with her.

It might be a good time to sit down at the edge of the bed and look across the room (not so far, mind you, like five feet away) so that we may better put a face and body on the object of my desire, my traveling companion/girlfriend/lover, Anna.

Forgive me if I get a little carried away. You've got to understand that it's been a few days. Even though I'm tired and I know for sure that she wants to go to sleep right away, I still can't quell the eternal optimism I feel at these moments, when we're finally alone after a party, a concert, coming home from work, or perhaps escaping the largest gathering of people ever on the planet, that she might throw herself at me or, more likely, that she'll come near me and I'll find some bare skin on the back of her neck to run my fingers down, run my hand through her hair....

Watching her unpack her stuff—what would she have in her bag?—camera equipment (she's a photographer), underwear, her "dopp kit" (a name I never understood for her black case of toiletries always bursting with soaps, medicines, repellent), raincoat, journal-scrapbook full of pasted-in train tickets, Hindi newspaper clippings, and fruit. There was always a piece of fruit that she'd bought somewhere or another, at the train station, from a vendor at the side of the road. Five rupees (about eleven cents) for a mango, papaya, pomegranate to tuck away into her backpack for later. She had this knack for pulling out a couple of perfect bananas at just the right time. Or forgetting those same bananas until two days later when they're discovered as a squished-up, festering jam at the bottom of her bag.

Besides the fruit, Anna could also roll her little body into a ball on the train or wherever we were and just disappear, fall asleep, make like a turtle with her big pack on, tucked away in the shell.

I was a big admirer of her many talents.

The downside—from a traveling standpoint—was her mop of

blonde hair. Blending in with the locals was not her thing. I can walk through an Indian marketplace without drawing too much attention. Sure, I'm very much a white dude, at least on the inside. But with my dark features, brown skin, and a swarthy beard I pass, at least to me, unnoticed. But with her at my side, my cover is blown. The hucksters and louts swarm. I guess they just don't see too many North Carolina born and bred red-state girls, complete with traditional southern family upbringing—grits, church, country music, the whole bit.

It's so hot in Khajuraho. She's in her shorts and a tank top. By now, she's probably noticed that I've stopped doing whatever I've been doing and am just staring at her, staring at her ass. She's bent over, unpacking—and I love how vulnerable my lewd, penetrating gaze can make her feel.

Tonight, she's got barely enough energy to wash up and crawl into bed and now she's wary of coming within arm's distance of me. She frowns.

"No," she says.

Anna is lying on top of the bed with no covers, with hardly any clothes. And I would maul her right now, but for tonight I'll be reverent and not put up a fight and let her sleep, because travel hell has taken a toll on us both and I don't know any other girl who could make it through what she has recently done without freaking out or getting sick or hating me for dragging us into this insane mess.

Tomorrow is a big day. We've got to get up before dawn to catch the "magic hours"—photo geek-speak for that span of time encompassing dawn, when the light is diffused and (on a good day) everything looks like an Impressionist painting. It's a time of the day I don't see quite as much back home, now that she's done moved back to grit country and left her Yankee boy all alone. Yee-haw.

Of course, I couldn't see all this (the subplot, the future) sitting across the room from her in our Khajuraho hotel room. At this moment and time, I'm resting on my side; arm up under my head, the future and everything else in my field of vision obscured by the rising and falling undulations of breasts. Future be damned.

Lying on that bed, my little untouchable—I wanted to tell that girl so many things. For every reason she's got not to fuck, I've got thirty why we should. My mind is a fucking supercomputer, with carnal energy fueling all my circuits, firing off crazy thoughts. All I want to do is tell her that two people like us could get together and tear each other apart, and give each other everything they'd ever wanted and make the rest of the world seem like nothing, and then go even beyond that, like how we could go to India and...if I somehow said the right incantations she might realize there's no point in giving into the pettiness of sleep deprivation, start pulling off her shorts, or at least touch me, if only to get this interior monologue to shut up and mercifully allow me to fall asleep.

Our 5:30 A.M. call-time arrives with a beeping travel alarm. She's in my arms, still mostly naked. In a few hours it'll be stifling hot again, but right now the warmth of another body feels so perfect. I'm clinging to her, my chin nuzzled in her neck, my leg wrapped over hers, my clenched hands under her shirt, full of breasts. She springs out of bed with me tugging at her tank top. I watch as she loads fully charged batteries into the empty camera, threads the film, looking out the window. And I say, "Come on, babe, come back to bed."

But this photographer isn't going to open her shutter for me, not even for 1/1000 of a second, even though I've got my telephoto lens zoomed out just as far as it can go. Not with all that beautiful light outside, she won't. If I don't get up and put my boots on she'll be out the door and I'll be on my own all morning. Just me and my telephoto lens.

The town of Khajuraho itself is not much to look at. Some hotels and restaurants and vendors on every corner hawking the standard tourist schwag. The aforementioned jungle, once demurely hiding away the temples, is long gone. It's dusty now, with only a few trees dotting the landscape.

Actually, I really dislike the place at first because I'm still going through that momentary girlfriend-turned-me-down-I'm-left-with-my-dick-in-my-pants grumpiness. But my scowl is short lived. There's nothing sexier than watching her snap pics, pausing and contorting in some crazy angle, bending down and sticking out that rump again. And my indefatigable sprits are raised because I'm watching her, knowing that eventually she will open up her body to me.

Walking up to the gates where you buy tickets to enter the temple complex, we encounter an old man with a few piles of fruit set out before him. She buys a couple of mangos and sticks them in her backpack for later.

The temples are spread out over a few square miles in the complex, and you can spend all day, if you want, hiking from one to another. Since light is our modus operandi, we head straight for the main temple to catch it right at dawn.

From a distance, it looks like your standard, millennia-old stone temples with steps leading up to a thirty-foot-high entrance peaked with carvings of various Hindu gods. The sort of archeological marvel that you get terminally bored with after a week of touristing. Nothing special until you get closer. The devil is in the details.

These temples are covered inside and out with sex. Over a century of work by master stone carvers, creating thousands of swarming representations of sexual congress in all its myriad possibilities.

Right away, we come upon a temple baring many positions of (apparently) the Kama Sutra. One of the most infamous carvings is of a woman, legs splayed in an acrobatic split, held by two servants above a man who is servicing her from an impressive, upside-down, shoulder-stand position.

Got all that? Best to stop for a second, close your eyes, and try to imagine yourself doing it. It's more fun that way, really.

Almost everywhere are sculptures of curvy temple prostitutes with big, round, fake-looking breasts. Huge breasts. Balloons. Taut, erect nipples. Every female carving here is the Indian embodiment of Pamela Anderson.

Not every carving is sexual in nature, but sometimes you just have to look closely. On one wall there's a seemingly tame military scene: An army marches in relief around the base of a temple, soldiers leading their horses. The scene is probably forty feet long, but it you look closely you'll notice one of the soldiers toward the end of the line is leading his horse from behind—his big dick sticking right up the horse's butt.

Some of the temples have been reduced to rubble, but on others the bulk of the carvings seem in pristine condition and probably look the same as they did back in the days when they were used for…well, whatever they were used for. Erotic or otherwise, these are some of the greatest masterpieces of Indian art.

Standing at the foot of these epic shrines to lust, you can't stop thinking about what it must have been like, what kind of people would have built these temples, what sort of lives they led, and the liberal and ecstatic fucking they must have done. Or maybe they just daydreamed a lot. Or maybe it was all some sort of crazy test of will (kind of like me this morning)—voluptuous temple dancers laid out naked on altars waiting, begging, to be serviced by meditating monks following their painful vows of chastity.

Whatever it is, one thing seems obvious to me—whoever was behind building these temples wanted a permanent record of human coupling. As if fucking were an art that somehow could be forgotten and they wanted to make sure, somewhere deep in India, that even if everything else was erased, there in Khajuraho would remain a permanent archive. So aliens can land here one day and see that female humans had tits bigger than their own heads and copulated standing on one leg.

And even though it's all lifeless stone, there's a sensuality to running one's fingers over the contours of the carvings, over the breasts, running one's fingers into the notches where the stone hips of a man and of a woman cleave together in eternal thrust. Obviously, the sculptures are tame by today's porn standards, but more tactile than a painting, magazine, or movie.

I don't know how long it took for someone a thousand years ago to carve something like that. Just one of these figures—maybe a week, or a month? But I like the thought of breaking sex down so slow, to take a month to freeze-frame one second in time. To think about one breast for a week. Anna probably wants me to stop staring at her now—it's making her nervous—but she should know that I need to see her vulnerable like that sometimes, that there's nothing she can do to stop me from looking at her except for learning to stop feeling so vulnerable when I look at her like that. It's the kind of thing that should be so easy to figure out, but in practice it isn't, which (I think) is part of what makes sex so complicated and wonderful.

Here's another idea—maybe Khajuraho was home to the porn-viewing booths of their day. Pay an attendant for a ten-minute time slot, go in, look at the carvings, all the girls with gigantic breasts, and do your business. Or maybe they were casinos. Or maybe Khajuraho was a horrible place—torture, sacrifice, rape, slavery.

Away from the main temples we come upon smaller, less-adorned structures. Anna and I happen upon one, smaller than the rest, with no windows or pillars or open walls. Even in daylight, the sun only casts light in the door a few feet, and then the space recedes into pitch darkness. Sort of gothic meets Egyptian tomb. Flashing a camera in there momentarily reveals an ominous, black sculpture on the back wall.

It's not a big room, maybe thirty feet deep. Much smaller than the other temples. We stick our heads in and try to get our eyes adjusted to the light. But it's vastly dark, and instantly we can feel how nice and cool it is inside, so we're drawn in, stepping in slowly as vague shapes take form and our eyes adjust to spy, not only this sculpture in the back, but also an altar in the middle of the room. Flat, rectangular, long, perfectly smooth, the kind of surface you expect to run your hand over and feel the stickiness of sacrificial blood.

We're running our hands over the rock, feeling the textures, the jawbreaker nipples, stone divots for belly buttons, and peach-pit sized testicles. Where the male member is deeply embedded within a temple dancer, the artists are always sure to add a low-hanging sac close behind for anatomical verisimilitude.

We take cautious steps, moving toward the altar, stepping all the way into the darkest part of the temple. We run our hands over the altar. Cool. Smooth. And I want to touch Anna, and ease her back onto that altar. And I imagine, a thousand years ago, moonlight streaming in through that door and torches flickering, throwing light in frantic shadows across the rocks, revealing a manic array of sexual positions, surrounding you everywhere in your field of vision. I think you can't truly understand the power of this place during the day, kept sterile and safe for tourists. At night I think there would be incense, drugs, flowers, the sounds of the jungle—birds, bugs, howling monkeys, tigers, snakes. The kind of place where extreme Hindu sects practiced the left-handed path—that of those who believed that human sacrifice, cannibalism, rape, bestiality, and more was the path to immortality.

It starts to give you an idea of the power of this place, what this city of sex temples may have been, or not.

It's one of those things, I think—you come thousands of miles to India, and then by trains and a Jeep over all that dangerous rocky road risking life and limb, and after all that effort, shouldn't you do it in the sex temple? You're there with your lover, and no one is saying your life is going to change or that magic will happen or that the telluric currents created by simultaneous orgasms will be amplified by the temples, detonating in an atomic blast that blows Khajuraho clear off the map. I don't even know if it'd necessarily be good sex, knocking against hard, cold stone for the sake of fucking in a fuck temple. But still (at the risk of sounding whiny), isn't that something you just do? Being good tourists? Something to write about later? A story for the grandkids? What are the chances someone would walk in? It's early in the morning, most people are still in bed. So why not even just a quickie?

Back in our room, she pulls her camera bag off her shoulder, plugs in the recharger for the battery, and then turns to me, walks toward me, presses up against me, leans her weight against me, tilts her head up, and parts her lips slightly so that as I lower mine, I feel—or taste—the hotness of her breath first; it hits the back of my throat and I freeze.

But it's so hot out now. We throw the windows open and there's no pretense about taking off our clothes. Not each other's clothes, just freeing ourselves from our own clothes as quickly as possible. Now I can stare at her, at the girl I'm about to fuck, and now she loves my eyes on her. She pulls out a pocketknife from my bag and reaches into her backpack and finds the mangos, considers her options, lightly squeezes each one to see which is the ripest. She chooses the bigger of the two and then, inspired perhaps by the temples, we sit up on the bed facing each other.

She's sort of sitting on my lap, thighs wrapped around my waist, her ankles locked behind me. A shift in my hips would take me right into her. But I can't help getting caught in the moment and holding off for a second, mesmerized by this angle, looking down between us, down at her legs spread wide open. If you think about it, with all the different angles from which one can view the female body, there aren't too many that give you such a closeness to lips, a full view of the breasts, and also—hips turned up to meet mine—a full view of spread thighs.

She opens the knife. I grab her ass for support and I'm pulling her toward me, holding her tightly against me, and then spreading her thighs wider, getting in closer, taking advantage of the control I have over her while she's trying to open the blade.

The knife is very sharp. It breaks the skin of the fruit and juice is dripping on our laps. I take a hand away from holding her steady, just for a moment, to rub the nectar into her skin, swirling it on her inner thigh, and then raise my fingers to her lips, letting her lick the first sweet taste off my fingers.

She is an expert at cutting mangos. She runs the blade around the circumference of the fruit, working the flesh free from the pit, separating it into two uneven hemispheres. Putting aside the pit-half, she cuts a grid into the flesh of the fruit, slicing five straight lines from top to bottom and five lines perpendicular, cutting through the tender mango meat but never cutting the tough skin, leaving it intact and holding it all in one piece. Sort of like a tic-tac-toe board.

Then she pulls the mango inside out. If you've never seen this trick before, imagine pushing a diaphragm inside out, or an umbrella getting flipped inside out in a heavy wind. With the squares sliced into the fruit, a grid springs forth. Blooming into luscious squares of nibbleable mango meat. Little nubs of perfection, dripping everywhere on us now, mixing with our sweat and that slick stuff that's coming from between her legs.

She selfishly takes the first bite, sinking her face into the fruit and then, smiling—because if there has ever been a "vegesexual," this is the girl, and she's euphoric right now with hard dick and soft fruit both at hand. Anna turns the golden nubs toward me, holding the fruit an inch from my lips, and I reach out with my tongue and lick away a drop of juice. I impatiently reach between her legs, push in deep with two fingers, and she moans to feel me inside her so suddenly, finally, rough fingers hooking up slightly and jamming back and forth once, ten times, twenty times, shaking her whole body. I hold her tighter and move my hand faster, just for a moment, until I withdraw my hand and run my fingers over her lips and she licks the taste of mango and girl. I kiss her deeply and then sink my teeth into one of the nubs and get juice and shreds of fruit all over my face. With the other hand, I'm still gripping her ass, holding her up in this position so she can feed us our breakfast.

And she's finally on her back and the future and the past and who she is and who I am are pointless because spread thighs are a reality and a universe all to themselves. And later on, when I'm lying in bed with my next hard-on and I'm thinking this is the best time of my life, I'm totally dissatisfied because there's still this thing unfulfilled: that I want this girl, and I want every millimeter of her body. And I'm never going to make her understand. And I want to make love to her in every temple in India, or at least in all the hot, sweaty, cheap-ass hotels nearby.

My Porno Life
Carly Milne

When the dot-com crash unleashed thousands of qualified individuals on the worst job market in years, I became a porn journalist. With the crisis of unemployment out of the way, I was eager to concentrate on my life as a working writer. For my first assignments, I watched my first S/M video (*Whip Her! Snap Her!* from Red Board Studios), screened a copy of Jenna Jameson's then-newest tape (*Briana Loves Jenna*), copyedited more dirty-talking prose than I'd ever read in my life, and went to my first porn set. As I drove to Encino, California, to watch a porn director orchestrate a hard-core film based on the story of Cupid, I found myself nervous about the prospect of watching two people do things to each other that are typically saved for closed-door, private enjoyment.

I tried to be quiet and blend into the background as everyone hurried around the set, prepping scenery and primping the film's starlet. But in an effort to make me feel more comfortable, her then–husband and scene partner invited me to pose with him in a photo. The result was a picture of me looking bemused and nervous as the smiling porn performer stood next to me in a tux, with his arm around my shoulders and his cock sticking ramrod-straight out of his fly. Mere moments later, the porn star couple were in a world of their own, locked in a passionate fuck, seemingly oblivious to the cameras and microphones and crew around them. Over dinner that night I excitedly explained the whole process to my boyfriend.

I soon settled into what was going to be a routine of porn journalism for nearly a year. Porn journalism wasn't the kind of writing I dreamt of doing when I grew up, but my comfort with sex, and the industry's sometimes unnerving comfort with it, made my "on the set" articles a breeze to write. Seeing a print piece with the words *cock* and *cunt* liberally laced throughout (and my name on the piece) was more fun than I'd imagined. But ultimately, all that porn viewing came to be my libido's undoing. I couldn't find the right words to say in my reviews anymore, and I was aware when everything I wrote about sex positions and ejaculation started to sound the same. I was starting to get extremely burnt out, to the point that when I'd watch porn on my leisure time, I'd begin aroused and end angry about clumsy lighting or amateurish dialogue delivery.

With in-the-field experience impossible to learn in any school, I took a job as a porn publicist at an adult movie production company. Strangely, I wound up doing more writing as a publicity/PR person than I ever did working as a porn magazine journalist. Not only was I doing box cover copy for some of the titles the company was putting out, but I also started my own website for people I knew to keep tabs on me and my industry travails, freelanced for a number of adult publications like *Hustler* and *Club,* and contributed my thoughts on the adult industry to various anthologies.

It seemed that I had found my niche writing about porn, but not everyone was as comfortable with this—or as jaded by it—as I was, which I soon discovered when I went home for Christmas one year. Some snippets of conversation that I experienced:

Somewhere in a mall...

Me: ...so then he had to go to the store and buy douche and enemas.

Her: Wait a second. What?

Me: Douche and enemas?

Her: What the fuck for?

Me: Well, before a girl does a scene she kinda has to prepare, so the enemas are for—

Her: Okay, stop right there. I don't need to know this. (Plugging ears.) La la la la la la la! I'm not listening!

At a pseudo-hip club...

Him: So what do you do for a living?

Me: Porn.

Him: (Choking on his drink) You...do porn for a living?

Me: No. I publicize porn for a living.

Him: Porn needs publicity?

Me: You think those tapes sell themselves?

Him: Yes.

Me: Well, you're right.

Him: So porn, eh?

Me: Yup.

Him: What's Jenna Jameson like?

Me: She's cool. She asked me to be the godmother of her first-born.

Him: Wow, really?!

Me: No.

Him: Oh. (Pause) Okay, so I have a question.

Me: Shoot.

Him: Well, see, my last girlfriend said she thought I'd do really well if I ever decided to, you know...so, like, if I wanted to get in the industry...

Me: (Walking away)

At a dinner party...

D: So what's coming up for you?

Me: Well, the Expo is right around the corner.

D: Ooh, fun!

Me: It can be. Or it can be intensely irritating, depending on the time of day and how enclosed your booth is.

D: I think it'd be great for people watching. I'm sure you get all types at something like that.

Me: Yes, that's one way of putting it.

D: You know what you should do? Take your mother! I'm sure she'd love to see something like that!

Me: Yeah...uh, no.

At the same dinner party...

Her: So where do you live now?

Me: Los Angeles.

Her: Fantastic! Are you still writing?

Me: Yep.

Her: What kind of writing?

Me: Well, it tends to be more sex-related stuff now.

Her: Oh?

Me: Yeah.

Her: I see. So what else are you doing out there?

Me: Porn publicity.

Her: (Pause) Porn?

Me: Yep.

Her: (Another pause) I'm going to go get some shrimp cocktail. Excuse me.

Needless to say, I learned very quickly to whom I could say the "P" word and to whom I couldn't.

Of all the bizarre reactions I got when I answered the question, "What do you do for a living?" I'd have to say the most bizarre and intriguing reactions came from friends, particularly those whom I hadn't conversed with since my career shift. Once, I spoke to a friend that I'd been out of touch with for a while. He knew about my job, as we talked plenty of times about what porn magazine journalism entailed, but after seeing my website and learning that I'd moved into a different role, somehow this changed his perception of the whole thing. "Wow, you're, like, totally into porn now in a big way, huh?" he said to me. "I mean, I knew you were interested in it before, but now...wow."

I was a little put off, contemplating what he might be insinuating, but I gave him the chance to explain himself further by asking what he meant. I didn't think that just because I'm a porn company's publicist and that much of my writing centers on the adult industry, then it must mean that I'm "obsessed with porn." He fumbled with a response, trying to pass off what he said as something that he didn't really say, but I knew what he was getting at. It wasn't the first time I'd run into this misconception: basically, that I must be completely consumed with pornography in all its manifestations, sex-obsessed, the cliché porn addict, or somehow sexually damaged, otherwise I wouldn't be working here.

Being compartmentalized with this stereotype only occurred more often as time went by, and continues to this day. Usually, somewhat repressed friends are behind the asking, because I don't think they can comprehend a girl working in the porn industry as actually wanting to do so unless something is "wrong" with her. I also don't think they understand that I got into the industry through a combination of accident and curiosity, which—as I understand it—is how a lot of people, in all aspects of porn, get involved. I didn't really seek porn out as a career, it didn't try to find me, but somehow, here we are. How does this translate into my being obsessed with the industry? Sure, I know the names of a few starlets, I recognize the names of different toy companies, and I can name at least ten titles that have been released in the last year. But that's part of my job. If a hairdresser can give you the hair color you're looking for based on a shaky description, does that mean he's obsessed? No, it means that he knows how to give the customer what she wants, because it's part of his job. If a woman tells her doctor that she feels a lump in her breast and he tells her it might be cancer, is he obsessed? Potentially, but my money is on the knowing-your-job thing.

But sometimes I wonder if it doesn't go further than that. Like, do they think all I do is watch porn all day, all night? Granted, watching a lot of porn used to be the primary part of my magazine journalism, but even then I was watching it in the office where it wasn't exactly cool to diddle myself. And burnout can be a powerful thing when it comes to one's horniness. As I said, when watching porn became more about how a scene was lit than the fucking in it, it had become a problem. That's not obsession, that's oversaturation.

The next question is always something along the lines of, "Well, did you get into it because you were having sex on camera?" Nothing against the performers in the industry, but why is it assumed that, because I'm a woman who works behind the scenes, I clearly got there because somebody dumped a load of spoo on my kisser in some numbered series? This insinuation has come not only from friends, but also from an industry lighting tech, and some guy whose house was a location I went to for an on-set publicity visit. Again, nothing against the talent, but I have to wonder: Is it really so hard for some people to believe that women can do things in porn other than fucking and sucking?

After they get over that learning curve about why and how this is my job, the next question is inevitably what the office environment is like. "Are there people fucking in your office?" they ask. "Do you work in a big warehouse and periodically people just start fucking for the camera?" Maybe at another workplace, but not in my office. I don't think people outside the adult industry get that—yeah, there's fucking and whatnot on sets, but the office is just like any other office. For example, the building I work in has a nice receptionist who greets you, a number of offices that each have desks with working computers from the present era, a mailroom with a copy machine, a lunch room, and boring bathrooms that have no glory holes. And while my office may look a little like a frat boy went in and decorated—lava lamp on my desk, skin mags strewn about, a novelty pussy-mold holding my writing utensils—I assure you that I sit at my desk and work a full day without anyone dropping by to ask me for a blow job. And likewise, nobody "services" me while I'm writing up purchase orders or press releases or doing whatever else I'm doing during my day.

I was talking with a director friend on this very subject, and he told me, "People don't seem to understand how boring working in the porn industry can be." And, in part, it's true. Sure, not every office in America hears discussions on whether or not you

can show that much "pink" on a box cover, and I don't ever re-
call watching a triple-penetration in the conference room when I
worked at Yahoo. But once you get over the initial shock and titillation of it all, it's just like any other job. It's a fun job—don't get
me wrong—but there are offices and paperwork and accounting
and whatnot just like in the "real world."

Springing my vocation on my friends and family was one thing,
but I was unexpectedly thrown into the uncharted waters of dating
when my significant other and I broke up. (And no, it had nothing
to do with the industry; our relationship just ran its course, as relationships often do.) I knew I'd have issues finding someone who
could hang with a self-assured, independent, confident woman, but
finding someone who could deal with the porn aspect as well and
wouldn't be either creepy about it or intimidated by it was surely
going to be a feat. That's why when a friend suggested trying one
of those "speed dating" things, I figured it would be a great way to
gauge Everyman's reaction to my place of business. After all, guys
in the industry were completely fine with what I did for a living; I
just didn't want to date any of them. And not only was I not paying for the speed dating experience, but I saw no harm in going
just to see if there were any cute boys capable of conversation that
didn't include discussion of their favorite utensil and which orifice
on the female body it looked good in.

Once I discovered that my friend and I were going to be joined
by a few other friends who also worked in the industry, I elected
to turn the evening into an experiment, of sorts. I decided to tell
every one of my potential suitors that I worked in porn, while my
friend would refrain from any mention of it. The end result would
be comparing how many people picked each of us based on the
information we gave them.

Of course, this also served my need to turn the event into

perverse theater for my own entertainment, but that's beside the point.

This installment of HurryDate took place at Gotham in Santa Monica, a cool little bar placed directly across the street from the Guess store, which lured me into its fitting rooms despite my greatest efforts not to shop. After buying absolutely nothing, my friend and I grabbed a quick bite to eat while we waited for everyone else to arrive. As we killed time till the night got started, we discussed the helpful icebreakers that were listed on our scorecards. You know, cliché lines like "Your ex: stay friends, or stay away?" or "Exercise: treadmill or remote control?" We agreed that they were lame.

"I think I'll ask people if they enjoy a funnel up their ass," one industry pal said.

"Better yet, ask them how they feel about ATM," I told him. "Then see how many people think you're talking about bank machines."

He started laughing. "How do you feel about anal on the first date?" he asked.

Awesome, I thought. I had my icebreaker question.

It was then that the host of the evening, a Stepford Wife–ish looking blonde with a whistle around her neck, gleefully called for all the HurryDaters to join her in the front bar.

"She's like the head camp counselor," my friend said as we plugged our ears so the shrillness of her voice wouldn't make us go deaf by the time the evening was through.

We all took our seats. My friend and I shared a table and agreed to stick to our plan. The camp counselor barked orders with a perk usually reserved for caffeine addicts or Kathy Lee Gifford. And with a tweet of her whistle, we were off. And now, a smattering of the most memorable moments of my evening:

Him: So what do you do for a living?

Me: PR for porn.

Him: (Pause) Really?

Me: Yes.

Him: Does the porn industry really need PR?

Me: Can you name me the last movie Jenna Jameson released?

Him: No.

Me: There's your answer.

Him: I don't know whether or not to believe you.

Me: What, you think I'd make this shit up?

Him: Well, I dunno…I met you, what, two seconds ago?

Me: Believe me, if I were going to make something up, it would be something that didn't include decoding industry terminology such as ATOGM.

Him: What's that?

Me: Never mind.

TWEET!

Him: I work in entertainment. What do you do?

Me: I work in entertainment as well.

Him: Oh yeah? What facet?

Me: The blue facet.

Him: (Whispering) Adult?

Me: Yup.

Him: Wow, that's interesting. What do you do?

Me: Just blow job movies.

Him: (Long pause, face starts to flush) So…you're…a porn star?

Me: Yep.

Him: (Sitting back in his chair) Really?!

Me: No. I do PR.

Him: (Somewhat dejected) Oh.

TWEET!

Him: So what do you do for a living?

Me: PR for porn.

Him: Really?

Me: Why does everyone think I'm making that up?

Him: Well, it's not something you run into every day.

Me: It is if you live in the Valley.

Him: Good point. So, how'd you get into that?

Me: Total fluke. I answered a job posting for *AVN*, and then I went to work for Metro as their publicist. Ron Jeremy is their contract boy.

Him: Ron Jeremy...man! Does that guy still do porno?

Me: Kinda. He tries, at least.

Him: He's gotta be the ugliest guy I've ever seen. He's, like, the Penguin from *Batman Returns*.

Me: (Gales of laughter)

TWEET!

Him: And you?

Me: I work in porn.

Him: Doing what?

Me: PR.

Him: Tell me about fetishes.

Me: What about them?

Him: What kinds are there?

Me: I dunno...you name it, it's likely a fetish.

Him: Well, like, what kind of fetishes have you seen?

Me: Foot, natural breast, young girls…

Him: No, like weird ones.

Me: I don't know that I find anything that weird anymore. I'm incredibly jaded now. Even the video I had to review that featured a naked chick rubbing herself with balloons for an hour doesn't seem that strange anymore.

Him: What about those people who dress up in costume?

Me: Oh, furries?

Him: Yeah!

Me: That's so last year.

Him: (Spilling his drink all over the table) Oh damn…hey, I got you wet! Ha! Get it?

Me: (Rolling eyes)

TWEET!

Him: So what do you do for work?

Me: Porn for PR. No, wait, that came out wrong. PR for porn.

Him: Do you get dental with that?

Me: What, did you just finish watching *Grosse Pointe Blank*?

TWEET!

Him: So, are you entrepreneurial in nature?

Me: You could say that. I work for myself.

Him: Doing what?

Me: Porno PR.

Him: Really? Wow, that's adventurous. I'm adventurous too. In fact, I at one time considered getting into the industry myself.

As a performer.

    Me: Uh...huh.

    Him: Really, because my adventurous nature...

    Me: (Silently praying for the whistle to blow)

TWEET!

    Him: So, how's your night going so far?

    Me: Really well, actually. And yours?

    Him: I'm having fun.

    Me: That's good. What's the strangest question you've been asked so far tonight?

    Him: I haven't had any strange questions.

    Me: Do you do anal?

    Him: (Long pause) Uhm...like, how do you mean?

    Me: Y'know, give or receive?

    Him: Ahh...I guess it would depend on the woman?

TWEET!

Another fifteen or so guys later, and we were done. And though my friend never told anyone that she worked in porn, our table got labeled "The Porn Table." And I also never wound up meeting someone of substance that night, either. I suspect they were all too freaked out by my vocation.

I don't regret taking work in the adult industry. In fact, I think it's become a tremendous asset in the world of dating. After all, there may be no greater litmus test for maturity than telling people you work in porn—and this fact has actively weeded out members of my family whom I didn't want to talk to anymore anyway, in addition to some fair-weather friends. The people who know me know that what defines the person I am isn't the stigma that surrounds what I do for a living. And as time goes on, I cherish them more and more for not looking at me as an oddity, but rather embracing this small segment of my life as one of the charming aspects that makes me who I am.

Now if only I could convince some of them to become anal queens on camera.

Just kidding.

Sex with Storm Troopers
Annalee Newitz

It's 1 A.M. Saturday, Labor Day weekend. Slightly intoxicated, some friends and I wobble into the basement of the Atlanta Hyatt and find a roomful of big, soft chairs facing a small stage. About ten people are in the room, some of them dressed like medieval peasants, most of them with guitars in their laps. A man in the back of the room starts strumming his guitar. He's the quintessential nerd: coke-bottle glasses, unstyled hair, a large belly. He sings a song about the days when giants walked the earth, when everyone was peculiar and it didn't matter.

We are somewhere in the bowels of the science fiction convention DragonCon. We are attending the Open Filk—an open mike gathering at which people perform science fiction–themed songs, often set to familiar tunes.

It's so cheesy that at first my friends and I giggle uncontrollably, covering our mouths and wheezing to hide our too-obvious rudeness. But then the deeper meaning of the song starts to sink in: It's mournful and sincere, a tale sung by an outcast aching for acceptance. The land where the giants walk is a place where geeks can hold their heads high, a place where difference is respected rather than punished. This filker is singing the deep-geek blues.

After listening to several more filkers, I get up to leave, thanking the guy who sang about giants, on my way out. His irony-free self-expression might be alien to my more cynical universe, where sentimentality has become a form of mockery. But I'm beginning to wonder if he's what I'm seeking—the core of truth beneath DragonCon's veneer of commercial science fiction hype.

Often called the biggest science fiction convention in the United States, DragonCon attracts more than 20,000 people to the Hyatt Regency and Marriott in downtown Atlanta every year for a three-day orgy of SF fandom. Giant exhibition halls are packed with people selling everything from rare 1960s Lois Lane comic books and pirated Japanese anime, to the latest role-playing games (RPGs) from White Wolf. Attendees spend their days at hundreds of panels learning about the finer points of fandom: how to speak Elvish, dress like a Klingon, rediscover old comic book favorites, or identify the specialness of each doctor in Doctor Who.

The main competition for DragonCon on Labor Day weekend is WorldCon, a literary SF convention featuring appearances by "respected editors" and postmodern writer-brainiacs like Samuel Delany and Cecilia Tan. DragonCon, on the other hand, is lowbrow by comparison. The keynote speaker is bad boy Harlan Ellison. The scene? A bunch of "tracks" devoted to *Star Wars, Star Trek, Xena,* and *Buffy the Vampire Slayer.* A special midnight session is dedicated to Internet porn. Gore special effects wizard Tom Savini promises to sign pictures of himself wearing his signature "cock and balls" pistol, featured in the splatterfest movie *From Dusk 'Til Dawn.*

Of course, I had to go to DragonCon.

Only there, hidden under the slag heap of pop cultural debris, could I find the savage, romantic heart of fannish geekdom: the people who wail out the blues, not the ones who hawk trinkets for cash.

It's almost a cliché to point out that SF, despite its progressive, utopian impulses, has for the most part sold out. Heroes are action figures; the quest for social justice is a high-concept Hollywood pitch; loving the alien is a pop song from the 1980s. Looked at from this perspective, DragonCon represents the commodification of every fan's dreams. Here, speculative worlds are equivalent to the dollars you pay for your fannish T-shirts, comics, swords, buttons, videos, DVDs, CDs, whatever.

All weekend long, I hear people griping about where their money is going. If, like many, you register for the con on-site, the cost is $75 per person for the whole weekend (preregistration and one-day passes are cheaper). Rumors swirl that some of that money is lining the wrong pockets. "All that money should go to staff!" a con-goer points out to me stridently as we wait in an interminable line to register. Looking at the tired, overworked staff, I have to agree. Are there no unions in Middle Earth?

Each "track" at the conference seems organized around some kind of franchise, complete with a new sales pitch for its latest trinkets. The *Star Trek* track whets con-goer appetites for the new "Enterprise" series; a *Lord of the Rings* track features a panel with scenes from Peter Jackson's big-budget flick; the *Star Wars* track has a LucasFilms spokesperson explaining why everything in the series has led up to the inauspiciously titled offering *Attack of the Clones;* a local Atlanta UPN affiliate has a big sign advertising *Buffy the Vampire Slayer's* resurrection in October; even the gentle Pernies from the Weyrfest are selling books and T-shirts from Anne McCaffrey's *Dragonriders of Pern* series.

People aren't here just to swap tales of great RPG campaigns and talk in hushed voices about why they adore Willow from *Buffy*. The hungriest among them are trying to "make connections" and get that elusive book deal with top-level SF publishing house Tor, or write a fantastic new world for White Wolf. Sure, they love SF. But more than that, they love money and fame. They're here to buy and sell.

But why would SF fans rejoice in the corporate control of fantasies they've nursed from childhood? The answer, like so many things at DragonCon, comes to me in the form of a story that unfolds right before my eyes.

When my companion, Charles, and I arrive Thursday night before the con is in full swing, we settle into the Hyatt bar and spend a few bored minutes watching TV.

Just then, our extremely drunk friend Kelly arrives. She's wearing a giant Nascar T-shirt on her diminutive frame, and has brought a "Mundane"—a nongeek, nonfan—along with her. He looks shaken.

"Hey, guys," Mundane says to us in a sweet Georgia twang, "I just met her in a bar and we've been having a really weird conversation." Kelly ignores him and looks me over. Hands on hips, she declares, "I want to kiss you. I want to stick my tongue all the way down your throat." Mundane starts to get pale, then he manages to stammer out, "I'd pay to see that!"

Some goths behind us grin and light a clove cigarette. When Kelly and I start making out, Mundane hands us each a $20 bill and speeds out of the bar. Settling into some new seats along with a handful of *Trek* junkies, we exchange perplexed glances. We thought he was just kidding about the money. It's so hard to understand the strange ways of Mundanes.

"Maybe he thought we were about to do a strip show or something?" Kelly wonders. The Trekkers have seen the whole exchange, and join our conversation.

"People used to say I had the best ass in fandom. I could wear a standard Star Fleet uniform when I was younger," says Joe, one of the Trekkers. "But now I have to wear the Riker uniform—you know, big shoulder pads to hide my belly." Joe has been attending SF cons for thirty years.

I stare up at the vaulted ceiling of the Hyatt and wonder how much money Joe has spent on Star Fleet uniforms in his thirty years on the USS *Enterprise* of the imagination. What's more tragic? Paying two women to kiss (a recognized Mundane ritual in strip clubs), or paying to live in a fantasy world where spaceships can take you far, far away and women kiss because they want to? Both are equally tragic, I think, but a fan's willingness to exchange money for fantasies is an understandable method of self-defense against a culture that doesn't understand her. Money, after all, is power. Science-fiction and fantasy commodification allows (middle-class) fans to escape from the horrors of Mundane life on a regular basis.

Selling out becomes a form of protection. If people will pay to live in your fantasy, that fantasy will survive a little longer.

Behind me at the Hyatt bar, a group of gamers are meeting for the first time.

"This is Jim, who invented the Krathgar universe," one of them says.

"And this is Kathy, who invented the Swiftriver universe," replies another. There is general murmuring, and several handshakes.

I decide to devote the next two days to getting the equivalent of a graduate education in fandom. Then, I'll work on getting laid. I start by looking over my program in the Hyatt bar, where I also have a good vantage point from which to study my DragonConian cohorts.

Klingons abound, and a veritable fleet of storm troopers are following Darth Vader. I spot a Cylon (gearing up, no doubt, for the new *Battlestar Galactica* series), a vampire, various fairies and goths, and a knight in full chain mail sharing a table with Daphne from *Scooby Doo* and Trinity from *The Matrix*. Strangely, there is even a Hunter Thompson look-alike smoking from a cigarette holder and chatting with somebody wearing an Atlanta Comicon T-shirt. I always knew Thompson was a geek.

There are also massive numbers of my fellow female nerds. Unlike at DefCon, another geekfest I attended recently, these women are not arm candy. People of all genders, races, sizes, and ages are mingling on the Hyatt main floor, wandering from panel to panel, stopping occasionally to hug or talk to old friends. Everyone at DragonCon hugs. It's one of the few environments where I've met strangers who ask me for a hug without a trace of sleaziness or New Age hippie smarm. Already, it's clear to me that DragonCon is more than a marketplace. It's a social testing ground, a place where people experiment with new kinds of relationships.

I inaugurate my course of study by attending an afternoon panel about how to bring horror into your favorite RPG. Run by three representatives from Hex Games, the company known for inventing the "quick ass game system"(QAGS), the panel quickly turns into a spirited debate about group gaming psychology.

"Personally, my ideal player is naked and on fire in a strange world!" enthuses Hex president Kevin Butler. He urges us to be imaginative, to become "partners" with our players and to remember that they need small triumphs even if they're eventually going to be eaten by aliens. A guy with a Cthulhu doll strapped to his chest in a baby carrier raises his hand and intones ponderously, "What players fear more than death is not knowing the rules."

The discussion turns to live action role-playing, or LARPing, where people don't just sit around and narrate what their character is doing, but act it out. We wonder if sometimes people take their gaming too seriously when they LARP. "I keep hearing about this Scandinavian website about sex during LARPing," laughs Butler, "and there's this big problem with staying in character while having an orgasm. Worrying about shit like that is going TOO FAR!"

It turns out that dozens of LARPs are going on at DragonCon, and I didn't even realize it. After the Hex panel is over, I chat with a player in the *Lord of the Rings* LARP, who is trying to entice new players to join in. She has a box full of envelopes with character names on them—you pick one, and can play the character for as long as you want. "There are more popular LARPs here, though," admits the *Lord of the Rings* rep, "and we have a lot of competition, especially at night."

Now, when I walk around, I stare more carefully at people who are in costume or who look like they're acting. Are they LARPing? I decide that if anyone creepy approaches me, I have the perfect excuse not to talk to them. I'll just flash a talk-to-the-hand sign and say disdainfully, "Excuse me, but I'm LARPing right now."

Later, I attend a Xena panel that features Katherine Fugate, the writer who penned the episode "When Fates Collide," a fannish favorite in which Xena and Gabrielle learn that no matter how their lives could have turned out, their fates would still have been tied together. It also includes some steamy girl-on-girl kissing. The large room is packed with women, many of them openly snuggling with their girlfriends. I'm smitten by them, moved by all these heartfelt displays of queerness in a southern state hardly known for tolerance.

Finally, a gray-haired woman stands up and asks the first question. She has a clear southern twang in her voice, and asks in the politest possible way, "What do you think of scenes between women in *Xena?*" We all know what she's really asking: She wants Fugate's opinion on the infamous "Xena subtext," the possible sexual relationship between Xena and her friend Gabrielle.

Fugate says simply, "I always thought they were lovers."

The entire room bursts into cheers and applause. Some women even stand up and stamp their feet.

Filled with elation, I exit the room and cross the hall to watch a roomful of *Buffy* fans putting on vampire makeup. In an environment where vampires, hobbits, and dragonriders can roam free, there is tolerance—even enthusiasm—for other kinds of difference as well. If Xena is queer, then why not hundreds of DragonConians? And if two strangers can get it on while LARPing, then surely casual sex is just another form of play.

At DragonCon, all eroticism seems to emanate from the Fantasm group. Fantasm is another Atlanta convention, much smaller, whose organizers are more interested in "speculative sex" than they are in *Star Wars* action figures. I find the Fantasm booth in the expo room with the help of Fred, a longtime con-goer who is an emeritus member of the Secret Masters of Fandom (SMOF), an Illuminati-style group whose covert email list controls the con universe.

The Fantasm folks are selling T-shirts that say things like KLINGONS DON'T NEED RIBBED CONDOMS, and pirated videos of Japanese live-action tentacle porn. Charles and I finagle a ticket to Fantasm's Saturday night party, which will feature Fred auctioning off naked slaves to partiers. "I also hear they're building a rack," Fred says conspiratorially.

Saturday night arrives, and Charles is dressed as Wonder Woman. I'm wearing my nicest *Men in Black* suit and tie. After having some drinks with members of Atlanta's queer SF group, Outworlders, I tangle briefly with some horny teenage boys who want to show me their swords ("They're really sharp! Can I have a hug?") and make my way to the Fantasm suite. The naked slaves are lovely; the cute young boy on the rack is turning a nice shade of red under a nerdy goth's flogger; and a foxy young game designer (why are they all game designers?) named Tony is ready to do whatever I want on the balcony. Some hottie who tells me he owns several comic book stores grabs me and we start kissing. Apparently, he helped organize Atlanta Comicon. So many luscious choices in my quest for sex!

But Charles and our friend Mehitabel decide that they absolutely must fuck a storm trooper in uniform. All weekend, we've been drawn by the fetishist outfits of the storm troopers: Swathed in shiny white plastic, their faces hidden behind imperturbable death masks, they make pleasingly mechanical sounds when they walk. They're like cars, or computers, or giant fascist sex toys. Rumor has it that they make their armor by hand, carefully cutting each piece of plastic out of a certain type of truck shell whose contours are well-suited for storm trooper conversion. The storm troopers' dedication to their appearance just makes them sexier. Not even Cindy Crawford works this hard to look good.

And so we leave the safe confines of the Fantasm party and run into the midnight hallways of the Hyatt, searching for storm troopers. Somebody at the Fantasm party has stolen one of the storm trooper walkie-talkies (yes, they're all in radio contact) and vows to help us out. As we begin our pilgrimage, we hear him sounding very official, intoning, "Calling all storm troopers. Report to the Fantasm party in room 931 at once."

On the main floor, we see two people in partial storm trooper outfits.

"Could you put your full uniform on for us?" Charles asks. Mehitabel giggles.

"I guess so," one of the troopers says uncertainly. "Why?"

"Well, we need you for sexual activities," I explain. "But just oral sex. See, we're at this party, and everyone really wants to have sex with a storm trooper. But you need to be in full uniform."

Both storm troopers are looking a little disturbed. "Why don't you try some of the other guys? They're downstairs."

Downstairs, we find more partially outfitted storm troopers. They look far less enticing with only the top half of their armor on. Each time we request sex, they send us to another part of the hotel. All the troopers seem to like the idea of putting on their full uniform for us, but when we bring up sex, they send us on to someone else. Don't they see the connection between their fetishistic uniforms and kinky sex?

"Storm troopers are all bark and no bite," a nontrooper tells us helpfully, adjusting her breasts inside a latex dress.

"They can't have sex in their uniforms because they're in command," Mehitabel replies mournfully.

But wonder of wonders, when we return to the Fantasm party for more groping, the walkie-talkie plan has worked. There are three storm troopers waiting for us, looking extremely confused. Unfortunately, they aren't in full uniform. After a long discussion about storm trooper design, we discover that the uniforms are like overalls—they're mostly one piece, and once you have them on, it's hard to lie down or bend over or, um, anything else. Sadly, the one trooper who is interested in debauchery doesn't have a hinge on his plastic storm trooper crotch guard, so we can't get access.

"What were you thinking?" I berate him. "How could you

make a uniform like this without hinges on the crotch?" I tap the thick white plastic over his underwear and frown.

"I'm sorry," he says, looking genuinely contrite. "I didn't have time." Another trooper proudly shows off his crotch hinge, but declines the oral sex.

"Hasn't anyone ever wanted to fuck you in uniform?" I ask the third trooper, who doesn't look very Imperial in his Gap khakis. Apparently not. We have reached the limits of our shared fantasies with these troopers. They're not going to play by our rules, and we're not going to play by theirs. I've learned another rule of tolerance at DragonCon: All LARPing is consensual, and if you find yourself in a LARP you don't like you can just go find another one.

Our storm troopers wander off in search of the Empire. Luckily, there are sexy goths, game designers, and comic book geeks aplenty at the Fantasm shindig. A slave feeds me some melon and then demands, "Do you think I'm only worth five dollars? That's all my master paid for me. And I even showed him my cock!"

And so it comes back to money, finally, the only social fantasy that DragonCon shares with the Mundane world. And yet somehow the science fiction fans who flock to Atlanta every year have managed to change the meaning of money to the point where it is practically unrecognizable. In Mundane life, there are no happy slaves. At DragonCon, every role is alluring because the whole social scene is treated like a game. Somehow, playing at life allows us to break the rules.

Sperm Bank Teller
Polly Enmity

I work in a sperm bank. I find it amusing to call myself a "sperm bank teller." It certainly makes my father feel less anxious about his little girl being around male bodily fluids eight hours a day.

Sperm banking is an industry of much mystery. In a recent article in a men's magazine, a gullible male reporter revealed the impossibly high standards some banks hold for their screening specimens. (Let us say that my bank is not considered one of the more selective facilities.) My favorite porn mag comic strip recently depicted a "drive-thru sperm bank" of such low standards as to accept anyone with testicles, even if his donation money is obviously subsidizing a crack habit. Neither of these extremes of selectivity is true in my place of employ: We mostly feature average-looking men of average intelligence who are keen on earning an extra $60 or $80 for jacking off.

One would assume, by all the media attention and uncomfortable giggles when laypeople discuss my place of business, that sperm banks are the big urban legend du jour. In fact it is horrifically rote and mind numbing, but it pays for my bourbon and eBay addictions. Allow me to debunk some dearly held sperm bank myths for you.

A typical day at the sperm bank

I have my very own sad, tiny desk. When I say "desk," I am being very euphemistic. I am relegated to a small Formica table, the likes of which are seldom seen outside a high school cafeteria. I sit in the back of the laboratory, just across from the donor rooms. My job involves greeting the donors as they come in, handing them some paperwork and a specimen cup, explaining the process of donation, and ushering them to the patently asexual exam-rooms-cum-jack-off-centers to do their duty. I thank them as sweetly as I can for their generous donations, then I whisk the babies-to-be to the main lab where an enclave of folks (whose native languages probably don't include the phrase "sperm bank") examine the specimens and prepare them for potentially eternal rest in a huge vat of liquid nitrogen.

I was sent to phlebotomy school so that I could draw donors' blood to perform routine STD testing. Since my workplace is cheap and constantly broke, I was given materials for an online correspondence course in venipuncture. This should make everyone who visits a medical facility very concerned about the training of the person aiming a syringe at your arm. Also relegated to me are many miscellaneous duties, including cleaning up spilled spooge and restocking tissues and lube. Overall this is a rather unsexy job, made even more so by the mandatory huge baggy lab coat forced on me. Vexing above all is my new boss, whom I call Avaricious Extortionist Queen Earth Mama, who usurped company funds for a facelift and takes a daily three-hour lunch break. My job is monotonous and easy, but it provides me with much time to make friends with the donors.

Being a diligent employee, on my first day I picked up a donor catalog listing of all our available men by their codes, with vital stats such as height, weight, and occupation. I saw this as my menu of potential partners. Ahhh, hidden benefits!

How to sell your genetic material through a brokerage such as mine

It's not about holding an advanced degree, though it may work in your favor. You needn't be physically stunning or belong to Mensa. Nay, all you really need is a wardrobe of loose undies. Successful peddling of your sperm is mostly about the temperature of your balls. See, sperm production requires the testicles to hang away from the warm body core to prevent sperm from frying in the vas deferens. And sperm production is not correlated with any other physical factor. You could be unable to get laid at the ugliest bar in town at closing time, but if you wear boxers, hundreds of women will fight over bearing your children.

It also helps if a potential sperm donor has remarkably few sexual partners (none of the male persuasion) and can handle the thought of homunculi in his image populating the lesbian community. A good number of sperm bank clients live in the same area, some even across the street from an "intended family." A donor's bumping into a mommy on a public thoroughfare is a realistic possibility, especially for women who live in the city in which their sperm bank is located.

Men who have sex with men are automatically nixed for "high-risk behavior." This stipulation makes no mention of monogamy, condom use, or disease status. Allegedly, this is a USFDA regulation. Avaricious Extortionist Queen Earth Mama makes much hullabaloo about these alleged "FDA regulations." Despite their apparent importance, she is unable to cite the publication (print or online) from which she gathered these guidelines.

"Sandra," I inquired during one staff meeting, post my breathing exercises and pre my vegan meal, "could you get me a copy of these FDA regs you've been talking about? I'd really love to skim them, for the sake of self-edification." Pretending to care about work is ever so useful when one is as expendable as I. "I'm sorry, Polly, those are confidential documents that only I am able to interpret for us. Just trust me, it says we can't take gay or bisexual donors." Avaricious Earth Mama is now an oracle of medical knowledge, even though she let her nursing license lapse a few months ago and cannot technically and legally supervise the activities of the business she currently owns.

I use the little-known method known as a "Google search" to investigate this matter myself, whereby I discover that these are not strict regulations, just highly espoused notions. Medical directors of each individual tissue bank are permitted to make their own decisions about this issue. My apparently homophobic boss has elected to bar from our bank men who have sex with men.

To further disqualify any perfectly good potential donors, Avaricious Earth Mama has invented a rule for our donors stating that they cannot have more than one sexual partner every six months. Once again, the alleged FDA regulations were cited.

"What if a donor has two consistent partners? Like, he dates the same two people all the time, and they only sleep with one another?" inquires the janitor, who I believe could competently run the whole operation without misappropriating company funds for cosmetic surgery. "That can't happen," Earth Mama insists. "None of our donors would ever do that." I wisely shut up.

Even with these rules about sexual behavior in place, donors are asked on every visit to let us know if they have any new sexual partners, and what exactly they have done: anal, oral, or vaginal; condoms or not; everything but how hot their experience was. I advise donors to underreport, unless they had an experience with a lady of questionable repute and feel that they need to be tested. After all, the real question is: "Do you need testing?" Not, "Did you have sex?" If a donor is using condoms, I'm frankly not very worried about his disease status.

I guarantee that every sperm bank in America wants more donors. And because many of us won't let you donate at more than one in a lifetime, we are rather competitive about herding the most qualified men through our doors.

The first screening step is a phone interview. You will be asked about family and personal health history, which tends to rule out most candidates. A strong family history of, say, diabetes or depression will disqualify you before you even cast your specimen into a cup. So will excessive drinking, smoking, or drug use—though the definition of "excessive" is entirely at the discretion of the person who interviews you. Some feel that being within a twenty-foot radius of secondhand smoke at any point in your adult life will ruin your sperm count. Others feel that, sure, you can occasionally have some marijuana/crack cocaine/recreational Vicodin and still maintain an adequate number of swimmers in the pipeline. Frankly, this judgment is rarely a personal bias and more often a matter of how desperate the bank is for fresh semen. The smaller the operation, the more likely they will overlook your "medicinal" marijuana.

The big deciding factor for selecting sperm donors is, predictably, whether they have an absurdly high sperm count. This has very little to do with the volume one produces, size of penis or testicles, or personal perception of virility and desirability, but it *is* dependent on time elapsed since the last ejaculation, the temperature of testicles, genetics, and plain old luck. Some donors with a track record of several hundred million sperm per donation can find themselves having a low-count day.

If you survive the sperm count gauntlet (and only 10 percent of potential donors can make it this far), you are, at my place of business, invited back for a chat with a woman who has no psychological or medical training whatsoever for a psychological evaluation and review of family health history. She will pass almost anyone, save one young man who cried at the prospect of putting offspring into the world who would not contact him. Technically, she is supposed to reject you for a history of genital warts or herpes, "too many" partners, or certain family health conditions. Despite these alleged conditions, I have seen many a potential donor come in with birth defects (for example, a man with a harelip who was later disqualified for this and several other genetic diseases he was found to carry), and boys she thought were "cute" got to enter the contract despite a history of, say, human papillomavirus (HPV).

The rule against accepting donors with herpes or HPV is as bogus as turning away gay and bisexual donors, if you ask me. Neither of these diseases is transmitted via bodily fluids, only by skin-to-skin contact. Since it's pretty well established that no donor skin meets receiver skin in the sperm bank, it should be of no concern to those admitting donors into the ranks of acceptable breeders. Additionally, it is nearly impossible to find someone who *doesn't* have HPV or herpes. Most sexually active adults have one, if not both.

Are the donors as cute/smart/tall as their descriptions say?

Unfortunately, I find sperm donor catalogs a bit euphemistic. Where the description would call someone "ruggedly handsome," the real face behind the phrase often proves "ogreish." Some poor

boys are merely described as possessing "nice eyes," which is usually code for "we're trying our best to find something nice to say
about his appearance. Please bear with us."

Certainly not every donor is a deformed idiot blessed with a
huge load of sperm. There are several attractive, fuckable men who
need some cash and yet aren't quite willing to become escorts or
exotic dancers for it. Think of sperm donation as "sex work for
men who aren't willing to play 'gay for pay.' "

Lesbians prefer blonds: what people look for in their donors

In my experience, the Aryan alpha male type is absolutely the
preferred donor. Blond hair and blue eyes are inexplicably popular.
Tall is always preferred, regardless of weight. I think because most
of the clients do not date men, they can't make sense of the weight
numbers. For example, 250 pounds is a stocky man, even if he is
6'5". No one seems to take this into account. I spend far too much
time reading online personals, so I can interpret height-to-weight
proportions, taking into account musculature and bone mass, if
photos are provided. Blue-collar jobs are suspiciously absent from
the donor catalog: Soil drillers and carpenters are not as in-demand
as scientists, therapists, dentists, and lawyers.

Some men are turned away because they are unemployed:
Women want to think of their donors curing AIDS and healing
sick kittens, not sitting on the couch in their (loose) undies and
eating chips. The ever-popular job titles of "film director" should
be interpreted as "marginally employed young chap who wears
the same shirt every day"; "small business owner" means "janitor"; and "student" means "I have no income other than my do-
nated sperm." Occasionally, our clientele will look for a particular
personality trait, astrological sign, occupation, ethnicity, religion,
hobby, or resemblance to a friend, partner, or family member, as

dictated by our office staff.

All the tactics for selecting a donor seem to be absurd to me. I mean, who believes that a lesbian couple combines gametes to make a baby who looks somewhat like both of them? Will a woman love her baby less if he isn't blond-haired or hazel-eyed? There has been, in my recollection, exactly one person who ever told us that she simply wanted a healthy man as her donor. This is what I would consider primarily important in selecting a donor, but hey, I'm just the office peon.

So...whose semen would you prefer?

Personally, I go for the biker leatherfag type, which is somehow in short supply in the sperm donor rosters. I've bent my rules a bit to accommodate donors who seem especially sexually promising, and I have made a point of getting my hands (so to speak) on the occasional member of "my type."

I sort of knew this donor outside the bank. We had several mutual friends, and something of a promised sex date at one point. Considering the lack of interesting job duties I had on my day's agenda, I suppose there was no better thing to do than take him into the examination room, draw his blood like I was scheduled to do, and suck him off. I thought I was being clever by cloaking my sex play under the rubric of medical professionalism, but our walls are made of particleboard and have no ceilings. I am positive that every person at work that day got an audio show. In fact, one of the other lab staff saw me coming out of the room remarkably disheveled. He looked at me, looked at my donor friend, and said very suspiciously, "I go lunch now." I have since made this blood draw/oral sex routine a regular part of my slower days.

Apparently, this is a very confusing industry

Some folks just don't understand sperm banks. For example, one woman thought that we detained the donors in the lab at all times, and she got to come to the office, line them up, and pick her favorite to impregnate her the old-fashioned way. Though it feeds my fantasy of working in a man-bordello, this is sadly not the case. Instead, we prepare frozen, quarantined specimens for people to use at home, in our office, or in another medical facility. We keep it clinical, and that's hot for only a few folks.

In an ideal world, everyone at the bank would know the basics of laboratory functions. For example, you can't just dunk semen into liquid nitrogen and revive it later, all intact and as peachy and viable as before. Sperm needs to be buffered with a clear glycerin solution, and even this process doesn't keep all the cells alive. Sperm also come back as zombies. I don't mean the carnivorous kind; rather, they are slower and less motivated than before freezing. I fear for the field of cryogenics if we can't even keep tiny sperm cells intact.

One of my bosses, Incredibly Lazy and Overpaid Earth Mama, had a shamefully simplistic idea behind genetics. She was trying to become pregnant at the rather difficult age of forty-six. Convinced that her ovaries were still perfect ovulatory machines, she proceeded to pick out donors she liked.

While I clandestinely knitted, I heard a shriek of "Polly, is donor X349 cute?" Incredibly Lazy and Overpaid Earth Mama wanted to use him for her little one. Of course, he was neither cute nor potty-trained, but my job is to validate people's choices in donor. "He's fine," I affirmed. "Any reason? Do you need a date?"

She tittered condescendingly, as if I would dare insinuate that a man could come near her sacred old vulva. "No," she chided me. "I want his baby! Well, I want his face for my baby. I want donor

K746's musical ability and D369's Latin blood." Her plan was to combine multiple semen specimens into one huge syringe, insert it into said holy hole, and hope that the combination of many sperm cells and her dear hopes for the appropriate arrangement of traits would result in a baby with qualities of all three donors. The old girl doesn't know that genetic material is not like mixing a drink: You cannot combine three distinct parts and end up with one homogenous capsule with the selected pieces of genetic information you desire. It's one sperm per egg, ladies.

One potential donor was incredibly confused about the paperwork we require. We ask all donors to complete lengthy descriptions of themselves (for example, favorite color, personality traits, exercise routines) to give hopeful mommies an incomplete but satisfactory glimpse of their baby's daddy's life. One question we ask the men about is their special hobbies or skills. Some examples of good answers include: "I'm a good painter." "I can assemble anything." "I'm great with kids." One poor chap felt it appropriate to tell potential sperm recipients that he has "a very nice, soft touch. I made my current girlfriend (who is 53!!!) orgasm spontaniously [*sic*] the first time I touched her." This was not the only reason he was deemed an unsuitable donor, mind you, but it certainly had ample impact to prompt us to deny him a job jacking off. (Oh, he also admitted that his motivation for donation was that "achieving the dream of being paid to jack off is pretty alluring." If you, dear reader, ever hope to become a sperm donor, do *not*, under any circumstances, admit to sperm bank tellers that you want to be paid to jack off. They know that. Pretend you love babies and you think infertile folks/lesbians/single women deeply deserve to have wee ones without connecting to a real, live man. That is the right answer. Fake some altruism! Or, if you are a rare, sincerely altruistic person, let us know!)

Some donors also find it very difficult to climax in the small rooms with lumpy futons for furnishing. We (well, okay, I) try our damnedest to keep the rooms relatively tidy, free of manly odors, and stocked with lube and tissues. Unfortunately, a few guys find it necessary to cover the futon with all the tissues in the box, use every packet of lube, and spill some of their donation on the floor. A few messy boys have been known to turn the rooms into their own personal porn-viewing booths for up to two hours. This includes cranking the volume on the DVD player so loud that it causes our receptionist to wander about, trying to locate the crying baby or wounded mammal. No, it was just Shaylenne having a good cervix-pounding on the TV screen of Room 2.

Is it better than unemployment?

No! I am currently "sick," watching daytime TV, writing this essay about the job I hate. One bonus is that sperm banks generally pay their staff well. I am paid far more as a sperm bank teller than I would have earned with my abandoned humanities Ph.D.

Surprisingly enough, there is a very low turnover rate in my sperm bank. Considering my coworkers' stated gender of preferred sexual partners, their attrition is unlikely due to the same reason I stay in the field. I can't say that "sperm bank teller" is one of those jobs that will ever be invited to junior high career day; the staff may wear lab coats and peer into microscopes, but most are merely glorified janitors. At least working here encouraged—nay, forced—me to finish my graduate degree, and it snagged me some hot stories for my own masturbation sessions.

Honestly, it's a pretty unattractive job. I touch bodily fluids all day. Donors faint when I draw their blood. Men hide packets of mostly used lubricants in our small, sweaty-smelling donation rooms. Part of my job description demands that I pick up these foil pouches without discarding the trash can liners, because we're too cheap to replace them more than once a day. I weed through magazine racks to discard the most lube-stained loose pages of old porn, feeling terrible that I will accidentally toss someone's favorite pink shot and cripple his future donations. I clean used vaginal specula with a foul-smelling, flesh-digesting enzyme solution. Most ludicrous is that I have four bosses (one for every two regular employees in our company), none of whom works more than three hours a day. However, I do get to spend more than half my day on the Internet, pretending to work, and screening donors as my potential sexual partners. I must say, I would have left long ago had my job not proven to be such a fertile source of orgasms.

Starfucker
Paul Festa

The ancients had a thing, Greek myth shows us time and again, for having sex with their gods. Since today's deities are elderly and asexual, look unkempt on the scale of the chronically homeless, or have been pronounced dead, we moderns have to make do with fucking the famous.

I chose a movie star. If I told you his name, you might quibble with "star." Perhaps, in terms of his career, he was only an asteroid or a Kuiper Belt object. But as an openly gay actor playing openly gay characters in openly gay movies, he had the heat and radiance of a supernova in my fantasy life. He wasn't mere celluloid jerk-off fodder, he was a plausibility.

My desire for plausibility was the first indication that I had moved beyond a normal moviegoer's fantasy life into the shadowy psychic and emotional realm of the starfucker. Not everyone qualifies for entry to this inner demimonde: Your self-esteem can't rise above the average film actor's crotch, and on some level you must secretly envy Monica Lewinsky and the late Princess of Wales.

In adolescence I showed a predisposition to starfuck. I was enthralled to learn that my parents had acquaintances who were even marginally famous, though these supposed stars typically belonged to the dim and dismal constellation of left-wing politics. My mother knew Harvey Milk! My father met Flo Kennedy! I collected autographs, a common and low-grade form of starfucking. An aspiring violinist growing up in San Francisco, I was a fixture of the Davies Symphony Hall green room, where I met visiting virtuosos after their concerts and dropped any name I could think of as they wearily signed my program. To what end?

In the spastic dance of misfiring neurons that passes for thought in the starfucker's mind (it more closely resembles religious faith), an interview with a third-rate movie star provided any number of perfectly reasonable escape scenarios from the mundane existence adulthood had foisted on me. The typical fantasy involved a sexually tense interview followed by passionate sex, then increasingly frequent visits to Los Angeles, introductions at Beverly Hills cocktail parties or orgies to well-placed friends in the business, a subsequent indiscretion or two with an up-and-coming director, and voilà: a dressing room with my name on it in the pantheon. Acting ability not required.

I caught up with my screen idol, sleazily enough, in a professional capacity. He was going to be at the local queer film festival promoting his new movie, and his career was just far enough below the radar of the mainstream media that I was able to score an interview without significantly exaggerating my credentials.

Too nervous to eat, I spent the final hour before the interview shaving so avidly that I cut my face in a dozen places and left my apartment bleeding, a wet paper towel pressed to my jaw. I had changed in and out of several outfits before settling on one that seemed to say *journalist with sloppy sexual ethics:* jeans, white T-shirt, black leather boots, and motorcycle jacket, a helmet of hair gel.

Ten minutes early, I was ushered into a tent behind the Castro Theater, a movie house that from the outside resembles a Mexican Catholic church and on the inside serves as a queer cathedral of star worship. Here, in the tent, I felt the closest approximation of divine revelation a gay secular Jew is probably capable of feeling. Rising from a red, curvy modern sofa, touching me with a lasciviously limp handshake, was the god incarnate, the spirit who could simultaneously manifest himself in houses of worship from Jerusalem to Santa Monica, in the waking and sleeping dreams of devotees around the globe. He was now concentrated (too concentrated—like so many film actors, this one was short) in unique, palpable, smellable, fuckable flesh. Throughout our interview, he ate a sandwich. I envied its entry into his body.

Because I am a compulsive personal archivist who once earned, from a bemused boyfriend, the nickname "Chronicles of Paul," and because I am a masochist, I kept the tape of our interview. Listening to it seven years later, I was pleasantly surprised by its professionalism. He came off smart, articulate, sensitive and funny, occasionally incautious yet somehow smooth. He spoke with affection for his theatrical family, told stories about the Islamic commune where he'd grown up and where adherents got a new name every seven years to signify the cyclical regeneration known as a *windu.* He had a background in painting. He read and knew something of the world outside Hollywood. Nothing he revealed about himself made me like or desire him any less.

For my part, I had prepared well, tracking down what few profiles and interviews I could find online, watching as many of his (mostly execrable) movies as I could rent. He had a lot of straight-to-video on his résumé, along with a healthy dose of gay film festival favorites, small roles in bigger movies, medium-budget horror. I asked a few frank questions, acknowledging the meagerness of his career. Did he think his being out of the closet and his gay roles had stunted it?

"I have no desire for fame," he replied. "I've seen, my whole life, what it does to people. I've seen how it affects their lives. They can't go anywhere without people wanting their autograph or wanting to fight them or fuck them or yell at them."

I took the comment as a personal reproach: Starfuckers were a problem, and I was part of it. But I needn't have taken it so personally. As the interview came to a close, his professional pose began to lapse. At one point, while I searched through my notes to make sure I'd asked all my questions, he snatched the pages from me and started reading aloud. I tried to get them back but he begged to keep them. Turned on by the spectacle of his pleading, inflamed by the power it bestowed on me, I relented.

The first few things he read were innocuous enough, but then:

"Typecast as gorgeous guys."

"Did I write that? I didn't write that."

"I'm sure."

"I can't believe you read that."

"I'm sooo sure."

Then the actor did something distinctly ungodlike: He became nervous. He fumbled with his things and stalled while I put away the tape recorder, the mike, the retrieved notes. He looked down, then back up again. He mumbled: "So, are you free later on?"

In the four hours of sex that would ensue in my nearby apartment, nothing would compare with the feeling of being asked, on the curvy red couch, by the god with nervous, darting eyes, if I was free later on. That simple question conveyed not just acceptance by a single person, but access to a world that in 1997 mere mortals paid an average of $8.50 to glimpse for ninety minutes at a time and could never touch with their hands or any other extremity. That question elevated me in status, put me on the receiving end of desire by an entity who existed to be desired. It put me, for a heady, hazardous moment, beyond the realm of the celluloid gods as the object of divine lust. And like other things that elevate you quickly—methamphetamines come to mind—this experience was never so heady as in the ascent.

From two in the afternoon until six that evening we smoked grass, sucked dick, wrestled, talked, listened to music, read poetry, smoked more grass, sucked more dick, and finally came—noisily, voluminously, spectacularly. He was skinny, well hung, butch and athletic in bed, much as I'd imagined him, but I experienced some dissonance between my expectations of the god-made-flesh and the reality I encountered. That marble smoothness of skin that revealed itself with such regularity in onscreen nude scenes turned out to be stubbly, marked by ingrown hairs. Those luxuriously full lips that, in the dark intimacy of the movie house, told of recent and imminent fellatio were, against mine, suspiciously lumpy.

But who was I to criticize? I was living out a fantasy. I was two stages into my starfucker's life plan (sexually tense interview, check…passionate sex, check…), and now I had to cinch the deal. Now, before letting him off this bed and out of this room, I had to make him fall in love with me. I went about this using a method I considered foolproof despite its never having shown the slightest evidence of success, which was to show him how culturally sophisticated I was by delivering, between blow jobs, learned disquisitions on the classicism of the Brahms piano *ballades* playing on the stereo, and the representation of dialect in the e. e. cummings poems I had him read aloud.

He endured these lectures gamely for a long while, then finally brought his index finger to my lips.

"Shh shh shh shh shh," he urged.

I became instantly mortified at my cultured logorrhea and apologized for it.

"I love being here with you, having you teach me things," he insisted soothingly, reassuringly. Then he turned me over and started eating out my asshole.

Generally speaking, I wasn't averse to having my asshole eaten out. On the contrary, I had vaguely romantic notions about it, thought of it as sort of a second or third date sexual practice. Sensing that I was going out on a bit of a limb, I said so.

Seven years later, I'm helpless to reconstruct the artful way in which his response implied, without spelling it out, that there would be no second date. Its meaning was clear, yet ambiguous enough that I could still construct labyrinthine starfucker life-plan detours around it. Those trips down to L.A. still awaited me, along with those cocktail parties and those indiscretions with directors. The fantasy life that survived the devastating oral–anal negotiation received a shot of pure adrenaline once we'd both come, showered, and dressed, and the actor wrote down his phone number, address, and his family's phone number so I could always get in touch. By the time I'd showed him to the door, disregarding the guilty, regretful look that seized his face as he said good-bye, I was convinced that I was all but officially Hollywood royalty by marriage.

"Believe that not anything which has ever been / invented can spoil this or this instant," read one of the cummings poems he had recited. The line would haunt me in the days and weeks that followed, which cruelly turned into months before I gave up waiting for him to respond to my letter or my calls, and then, absurdly, the years that passed before it didn't hurt to think about him, before I shook the feeling that I was hated by God.

My therapist at the time was useless. She wasn't interested in my confessions of starfucking machinations or the redoubled intensity of my desire for the actor. She just brought the story back where she habitually brought every story: to the subject of my abandoning, narcissistic father, his abrupt departure from our home when I was seven years old, and the scarring experience of calling him night after night, waiting in vain for my messages to be returned. All this upset about the actor had less to do with him or my evil, starfucking heart than with what Freud called the compulsion to repeat traumas in an attempt to master them through repetition.

How preposterous, to suggest that my afternoon of erotic epiphany could be reduced to something as common, domestic, and tedious as a Northern California divorce! My therapist was proving herself to be the one-trick pony of psychoanalysis. I considered putting her out to pasture.

But I needed her. The world outside her office was mined with painful reminders of my failed audition. Once you have starfucked, there is no stopping these reminders. A writer is said to have remarked about his marriage to a famous actress that it was "like fucking a billboard." The primary hazard of starfucking is that there is no divorcing the billboard. As long as she's still a star, you remain fucked. You're permanently involved. She's forgotten you, she's moved on to the next worshipper, and the evidence of your insignificance and her permanence is plastered on every highway, off every exit, on the sides of buildings, behind Plexiglas above urinals. A year after the interview, I came home from a two-week vacation and realized that in Europe, where my star is unknown, I had finally managed to stop obsessing over him. Then I turned the corner and saw his name on the marquee of the Castro Theater.

In my attempts to make peace with the encounter, I tried to take that cummings line to heart. Wasn't there something perfect and inviolable about that moment of invitation, those hours of sex? Couldn't they exist, under glass, unsullied by the foolish things I said and did afterward, the stalker-scented letter I sent in an elaborately painted envelope, the rambling, desperate voicemail destined to be deleted before it was heard? Some part of me persisted in believing the message that accompanied the invitation to his body: that I was special, elect, deserving of a god's desire.

That train of thought was quickly derailed whenever I committed the irresistible indiscretion of mentioning the hookup. The first person I told said, "Yeah, I know another journalist who did it with him." Another said he'd been responsible for driving the actor to a New York film festival, and wound up getting rimmed for a half hour as a tip. A third friend, in New York, mentioned that the last time he'd seen him, the actor had been fellating himself in a nightclub. I asked a mutual friend what the actor was up to and she put her hand to her mouth and her tongue in her check to simulate cocksucking. Far from feeling special, I now began to suspect that in my wider circle of friends, at least, the way to distinguish yourself was by *not* having sex with this particular actor.

In writing this reminiscence, I contacted him through that mutual friend. I wanted to finish the interview, ask him questions that had come up in the interim. Here is a transcript of our exchange:

"Do you remember having sex with me, or does it just blur in with the rest?"

(The actor declined to comment.)

"Are you aware of the power you exercise as a movie actor, and does it ever occur to you to use it judiciously?"

(The actor declined to comment.)

"How much sex do you think you get, just for being in the movies, on a weekly basis?"

(The actor declined to comment.)

"In a recent issue of *Star* magazine, someone says, 'If a friend of yours says they want to date someone famous, say no.' Good advice?"

(The actor declined to comment.)

In fact, the actor declined to be interviewed altogether. He declined to talk to me. This second rejection hurt like a pinprick on scar tissue; in seven years, more heartbreaks, and then a happy marriage, have covered the original wound in virtually impenetrable layers. I recently saw him onscreen and felt vaguely titillated that I had known the mortal body under those clothes and that makeup. I admired his performance. Mostly I felt a striking absence of pain or longing, and the impossibility of regret.

If a friend of yours says she wants to date someone famous, say maybe. Urge her to be clear about her motives. Thinking back on that afternoon seven years ago, I see two young men who wanted something from each other. He wanted something for four hours, and got it. I wanted the actor to change my life; I wanted to be rescued, plucked from the anonymous multitudes who had to fight for space and resources and love; I wanted to be transported to a place where there was no drudgery or obscurity, no real reason to feel sadness because the eyes of millions of people at any given time might be radiating love at your ubiquitous image. I wanted, that afternoon I went to bed with a person from the movies, no longer to be me. In a way that is only coming into focus seven years later, I got exactly what I wanted. I got what my therapist said I'd sought—repetition—and what all those poor nymphs got when Ovid turned them into fountains and shrubs and knickknacks to protect them from the lust of their gods: metamorphosis.

I had next to no acting experience, and less ability, and I wanted to be transformed into a movie star. Instead, I became a shrub. This came as a surprise, and a disappointment, but my fate was not without its consolations. Shrubs are immune to the poisonous desires of the gods. They are at peace with the circumstances of their provenance. They draw sustenance from the earth and sky equally. They are hardy. They grow.

Perhaps the moment we want to fire our therapist is the moment we are getting our co-pay's worth out of her. What does the starfucker want, after all? To accelerate his career. To accelerate his life. What does he get? In my case, I brought my life to a halt and hurtled through my *windu* backward in time, past the realities and disappointments of my career, past the recognition of an approaching adulthood that demanded an identity, all the way to the day I was seven years old and the only star in my firmament who would ever really matter went out.

About the Authors

HARLYN AIZLEY is the author of *Buying Dad: One Woman's Search for the Perfect Sperm Donor*, which appeared on nonfiction best-seller lists nationwide in 2003. More of her work can be found in *96 Inc., Berkeley Fiction Review, Boston Magazine, Mangrove,* and the *South Carolina Review,* as well as on FreshYarn.com. Her next book, *The Other Mother,* will be published by Beacon Press in spring 2006. Aizley's clay penises are on display in museums and art galleries all over the world.

TIMOTHY ARCHIBALD studied photography with Martin Benjamin at Union College in Schenectady, New York, from 1982 to 1985. He majored in art at Pennsylvania State University, studying with Marc Hessel, Gerry Lange, and Ken Graves. Archibald works as an editorial and commercial photographer, living in the San Francisco Bay Area with his wife, Cheri, two sons, Elijah and Wilson, and dog, Weegee. *Sex Machines: Photographs and Interviews* will be published fall 2005 by Process. The project has been excerpted in *Esquire* magazine in England, *Tease* magazine in the United States, and *FotoPozytyw* in Poland, and is part of the permanent collection of the Museum of Sex in New York.

PATRICK CALIFIA is the author of *Sex Changes: The Politics of Transgenderism*. He lives in the San Francisco Bay Area, where he has a private practice as a therapist. His other essays can be found in *Public Sex: The Culture of Radical Sex* and *Speaking Sex to Power: The Politics of Queer Sex*, both from Cleis Press.

POLLY ENMITY continues her travails and adventures in bodily fluids at a sperm bank she chooses not to name. She resides all by her lonesome, bitter self in the San Francisco Bay Area, spending much of her time further fostering disdain for the world around her. When she's not loathing, assisting donors, or writing, she is earning a master's degree in library and information science, fetish modeling, cooking meat, and training sex educators.

PAUL FESTA was born in San Francisco and educated at Yale College, where he studied English, and at the Juilliard School, where he studied violin. His essays and criticism have appeared on Salon.com and Nerve.com and in other publications. He is at work on an experimental music documentary and a novel, and lives in San Francisco with his spouse, James Harker, and their dog, Ziggy. His address on the Web is paulfesta.com; his hip-hop alter ego can be found at candyassrapper.com.

ELLEN FRIEDRICHS is a New York–based sex educator who teaches sex ed to teens in the Bronx as well as human sexuality at Rutgers University in New Jersey. She has written about sexual health for various publications and can be found at www.sexedvice.com.

MICHAEL A. GONZALES, a native of Harlem, has written cover stories for *Vibe, Essence, Code, Latina, Suede, XXL,* and the *Source.* His essays have appeared in *Rock and Roll Is Here to Stay; The Vibe History of Hip-Hop; Men of Color: Fashion, History, Fundamentals; Soul (Black Power, Politics, and Pleasure);* and *Vibe's Hip-Hop Divas.* Gonzales has published short fiction in *Ego Trip, Uptown, Russell Simmons' OneWorld, Trace, NY Press,* and *Brown Sugar (A Collection of Black Erotica).* He lives in Brooklyn.

CARLY MILNE's foray into adult entertainment began in 2002 as associate editor of *AVN* magazine. She then became the publicist for Metro Interactive, home of porn legend Ron Jeremy, and launched her popular website pornblography.com—which has won rave reviews, a stint on PBS, and an interview on the E! Channel's "True Hollywood Story" episode about Jenna Jameson. She writes for *Playboy, Club, Hustler, Penthouse, High Society, Fox Magazine,* along with writing porn scripts, and doing publicity for some of the industry's largest companies and stars. Her work has also appeared in *Bitch* magazine, *AVNOnline* magazine, and *Rolling Stone,* and she's been featured in the *Globe and Mail, Entertainment Weekly, Cosmopolitan,* and *Black Book,* among others. She lives in Los Angeles with her kitties, where she constantly attempts to shield her boyfriend from cat hair.

ANNALEE NEWITZ writes a nationally syndicated column about technology and culture called "Techsploitation," and her work has been published in *Wired, Popular Science,* Salon.com, Nerve.com, and the *San Francisco Bay Guardian*. She is also a policy analyst at the Electronic Frontier Foundation. Get the gory details at www.techsploitation.com.

CHRIS OHNESORGE has had more jobs since the age of fifteen than most people have in two lifetimes. From short order cook to guy-Friday, dot-com loser to sex club worker, he's done almost everything. A retail drone by day and a drummer in an indie rock power trio (Ex-Boyfriends) by night, he tries to squeeze a little writing out of his laptop in the spare minutes. Check out his queer hijinks online at www.ohnochriso.com.

ROBIN POSTELL grew up in her father's southern newsroom, affected by the small-town lives of backwoods lawmen and the doomed death-row inmates her father profiled. Drawn to extreme sports, she became a journalist covering the Ultimate Fighting Championship during the 1990s. She wrote about martial arts tournaments in the Ukraine and Kazakstan; eco-challenges in British Columbia, Australia, and Argentina; and the Marathon des Sables, a 150-mile, seven-day footrace through the Sahara desert. As her career developed, she began inserting herself into her fiction because "there really was no story unless I was part of it; that's what keeps me interested." Now editing her novel, *Underbelly*, Postell lives in southern Georgia.

CAROL QUEEN earned a Ph.D. in sexology after hearing a storyteller in the 1980s use the phrase "Follow what fascinates you." She's the cofounder/director of the Center for Sex and Culture (www.sexandculture.org) and the author or editor of many books, including *Real Live Nude Girl: Chronicles of Sex-Positive Culture* and *PoMoSexuals*. She's also an award-winning erotic writer. See a list of books and videos in which she's appeared at www.carolqueen.com. She lives in San Francisco with her long-time partner, Robert, and two nonpareil cats.

DON RASNER (a pen name) lives and writes in a small town in Indiana near Chicago. He is gradually getting over his superhero-ine fetish, at least until the next *Tomb Raider* movie comes out and reminds him of it.

SHIRLEY SHAVE is the alias of a porn actress living in Los Angeles. More of her story is at http://shirleyshave.blogspot.com.

K. ST. GERMAINE, aka Miss Satanica, is a circus sideshow per-former with more than three hundred shows to her credit and has also been a sex industry worker for nearly thirteen years. She is a Hollywood stuntwoman, is a spoken word performer, and does everything from light bulb eating to contortion. She has been fea-tured in the theatrical burlesque productions Lucha VaVoom, The Girly Freakshow, the Miss Exotic World Pageant, and Tease-O-Rama. Her television and movie credits include HBO's *Carnivale* (as a naked stuntwoman) and *Deadwood,* as well as the upcoming Bravo series *40 Deuce.* Her writing has appeared in several publi-cations, including *Tease* magazine, and she is also the mother of a thirteen-year-old boy wonder.

MICHELLE TEA is the author of one collection of poetry and four memoirs, most recently *Rent Girl,* an illustrated book with art by Laurenn McCubbin. She lives in San Francisco, where she curates, hosts, and bakes cookies for the monthly Radar reading series.

ARLO TOLESCO is a San Francisco writer and musician who has traveled the world investigating best-practices in both love and sex. He has published hundreds of articles on Yesportal.com and the Good Vibrations online magazine—and is perhaps the world's foremost authority on the subject of bad sex advice.

About the Editor

VIOLET BLUE is an author, editor, female porn expert, and pro-porn pundit. She has been a published sex columnist and trained professional sex educator since 1998, and she is the Assistant Editor at Fleshbot.com. Blue is the editor of *Sweet Life: Erotic Fantasies for Couples*, *Sweet Life 2: Erotic Fantasies for Couples*, and *Taboo: Forbidden Fantasies for Couples*, and the author of *The Ultimate Guide to Fellatio*, *The Ultimate Guide to Cunnilingus*, *The Ultimate Guide to Adult Videos*, and *The Ultimate Guide to Sexual Fantasy*. She has appeared on Playboy TV's *Sexcetera* and has been featured in such magazines as *Esquire; Adult Video News; Cosmopolitan; Men's Health; O, The Oprah Magazine;* Salon.com; and *Wired*. Visit her at www.tinynibbles.com.